Student Study Guide

GLENCOE Aviation Technology Series

Aircraft
Basic Science

Seventh Edition

Michael J. Kroes
James R. Rardon

GLENCOE
McGraw-Hill

New York, New York   Columbus, Ohio   Woodland Hills, California   Peoria, Illinois

Student Study Guide for Aircraft Basic Science, Seventh Edition

Imprint 2001

Send all inquiries to:
Glencoe/McGraw-Hill
8787 Orion Place
Columbus, OH 43240

ISBN 0–02–801815–X

Printed in the United States of America.

5 6 7 8 9 047 05 04 03 02

Contents

To the Student

This student study guide has been developed to accompany the textbook *Aircraft Basic Science*, 7th Edition. Its purpose is to help the student reinforce his or her understanding of the principles and concepts covered.

A series of *Study Questions* are intended for use after thoroughly reading each chapter. Many of the key points are covered in these questions to help the student review and better understand what has been read.

Application Questions will allow the student to apply mathematical concepts or to interpret and use other information presented.

A *Review Exam* at the conclusion of each chapter contains typical FAA examination questions relating to that chapter.

While many of the key points from the text are covered in the student study guide, it is impossible to include everything. You should not attempt to use this material as a substitute for a thorough study of the textbook.

It is suggested that the user first read the related chapter completely *before* attempting to complete the fill-in-the-blank questions. In this way, the completion of the fill-in-the-blank questions will both act as a review and reinforce the significance of particular discussions in the text.

The mathematical application questions, where included, should then be completed to ensure that the topic is understood. In most cases, these questions combine the most basic relationships into a single question. In some instances, questions relate to one another in order to demonstrate the interrelationships between different concepts. As a result, many mathematical application answers include short notes that anticipate common misunderstandings and explain in more detail the *Study Guide* answer.

Finally, for many users of this *Study Guide,* the primary objective is the attainment of an Airman's Certificate with an Airframe Rating. To assist in this effort, the *Study Guide* concludes each chapter with a series of multiple choice questions.

Chapter 1

STUDY QUESTIONS

1. The ten single number characters are called _____.

2. Our number system is called a _____ system, the name being derived from the Latin word *decem*, meaning _____.

3. _____ numbers, also called _____, are those that contain no fractions.

4. _____ is the process of combining the values of two or more numbers into a single value.

5. In _____ the number from which another is to be subtracted is called the _____, the number being subtracted from the other is called the _____, and the result is called the _____.

6. In multiplication the number to be multiplied is called the _____, and the number of times the multiplicand is to be taken is called the _____.

7. The answer obtained from a multiplication is the _____.

8. _____ is the separating or dividing of a number into a certain number of equal parts.

9. The parts of a fraction are the _____ and the _____.

10. A fraction whose numerator is less than its denominator is called a _____.

11. A _____ number is a combination of a whole number and a fraction.

12. In order to add or subtract fractions, it is necessary that the denominators have _____ values.

13. Multiplication of fractions is accomplished by obtaining the _____ of the _____ and placing this over the _____ of the _____.

14. The division of fractions is accomplished by _____ the _____ and _____.

15. A _____ fraction is a common fraction converted to _____, _____, etc.

16. To _____ to tenths of an inch the calculation would be carried to two decimal places.

17. The number of decimal places in the product of two numbers containing decimals will be determined by adding the number of _____ places in the _____ and _____ and using this many places in the product.

18. The principal rule to remember in _____ decimals is to place the decimal point of the _____ directly above the decimal point of the _____.

19. To convert a _____ fraction to a _____ fraction, write it in the fraction form and then reduce it to its _____ terms by dividing the numerator and denominator by the same number.

20. To find a certain percentage of a number multiply the number by the number of percent and move the _____ two places to the left.

21. A _____ is the numerical relation between two quantities.

22. _____ expresses equality between two ratios.

23. In a proportion problem the outer numbers are called the _____ and the two inner numbers are called the _____.

24. In a _____, the product of the _____ is equal to the product of the _____.

25. A small index number placed above and to the right of a number to indicate the _____ of the number is called an _____.

26. A _____ of a number represents the number multiplied by _____ a certain number of times.

27. The second power of a number is called the _____ of the number.

28. A _____ of a number is another number that will divide evenly into the first number.

29. A _____ of a number is a factor that when multiplied by itself a certain number of times will produce the _____.

30. _____ is the process of using powers of 10 to simplify mathematical expressions and computations.

31. An _____ is a mathematical expression of _____.

32. To add the terms in an algebraic expression when there are both _____ and _____ quantities we combine the terms with the same sign and then subtract the _____ value from the _____ and give the answer the sign of the _____.

33. In the term *3a* the figure *3* is called the _____ of *a*.

34. In algebra, letters used in place of numbers are called _____ numbers.

35. The rule for subtraction in algebra is change the sign of the _____ and _____.

36. When two terms with like signs are multiplied, the sign of the product is _____. When two terms of unlike signs are multiplied, the product is _____.

37. In solving an algebraic expression or equation, indicated _____ and _____ must be completed before _____ are made.

38. When a term is moved from one side of an algebraic equation to the opposite side, the _____ of the term must be _____.

39. Geometry deals with the measurement of _____, _____, and _____.

40. A point is that which has no _____, _____, or _____ but has only _____.

41. A line has no _____ or _____ but has _____.

42. A surface has no _____ but has _____ and _____.

43. A solid has three dimensions, _____, _____, and _____.

44. An _____ is the opening between two straight lines drawn in different directions from the same point.

45. A _____ is a closed curve, all portions of which are _____ from the same point.

46. A _____ is a plane, closed figure bounded by _____ joined end to end.

47. A regular polygon has all _____ and _____.

48. A _____ is a three-sided polygon with a total included angle of _____.

49. The _____ states that in a right triangle the square of the _____ is equal to the _____ of the other two sides.

50. A regular quadrilateral is a _____.

51. A _____ is a four-sided plane that has _____ parallel sides and _____ that are not parallel.

52. Area is measured in units of _____ or _____.

53. Volume requires that an object have _____, _____, and _____ and is expressed in units of _____ inches or _____ centimeters.

54. Trigonometric functions are based on the _____ of the sides of a _____ triangle to one another.

55. In trigonometry the ratios of the sides of a right triangle to one another are the _____, _____, _____, _____, _____, and _____.

56. Every number system has three concepts in common: (1) a _____, (2) _____, and (3) _____.

57. The _____ is the number of digits used in the system.

58. A number system known as the _____ system uses powers of two.

59. The _____ number system uses a base of _____ and digits from 0 through 7.

60. The _____ system uses 16 digits.

61. A _____ or _____ graph shows comparative quantitative data.

62. The _____, or _____, chart is used to graphically represent the division or distribution of a whole.

63. The _____ graph has a line connecting points that have been measured or calculated.

64. A _____ is a chart used for calculations.

Chapter 1

Name _____

Date _____

APPLICATION QUESTIONS

Part 1: Addition

1. 6 + 5 = _____

2. 4 + 9 = _____

3. 8 + 3 = _____

4. 7 + 6 = _____

5. 9 + 2 = _____

6. 5 + 8 = _____

7. 7 + 4 = _____

8. 8 + 2 = _____

9. 8 + 4 = _____

$$\begin{array}{r} 25 \\ +45 \\ \hline \end{array}$$

10. _____

11.
$$\begin{array}{r} 16 \\ +63 \\ \hline \end{array}$$

12.
$$\begin{array}{r} 34 \\ +64 \\ \hline \end{array}$$

13.
$$\begin{array}{r} 63 \\ +35 \\ \hline \end{array}$$

14.
$$\begin{array}{r} 75 \\ +44 \\ \hline \end{array}$$

15.
$$\begin{array}{r} 54 \\ +88 \\ \hline \end{array}$$

Part 2: Multiplication

1.
$$\begin{array}{r} 9 \\ \times 7 \\ \hline \end{array}$$

2.
$$\begin{array}{r} 7 \\ \times 8 \\ \hline \end{array}$$

3.
$$\begin{array}{r} 9 \\ \times 6 \\ \hline \end{array}$$

4.
$$\begin{array}{r} 11 \\ \times 2 \\ \hline \end{array}$$

5.
$$\begin{array}{r} 13 \\ \times 3 \\ \hline \end{array}$$

6.
$$\begin{array}{r} 13 \\ \times 7 \\ \hline \end{array}$$

7.
$$\begin{array}{r} 26 \\ \times 6 \\ \hline \end{array}$$

8.
$$\begin{array}{r} 73 \\ \times 7 \\ \hline \end{array}$$

9.
$$\begin{array}{r} 87 \\ \times 6 \\ \hline \end{array}$$

10.
$$\begin{array}{r} 86 \\ \times 9 \\ \hline \end{array}$$

11.
$$\begin{array}{r} 24 \\ \times 12 \\ \hline \end{array}$$

12.
$$\begin{array}{r} 38 \\ \times 14 \\ \hline \end{array}$$

13.
$$\begin{array}{r} 39 \\ \times 26 \\ \hline \end{array}$$

14.
$$\begin{array}{r} 93 \\ \times 67 \\ \hline \end{array}$$

15.
$$648 \times 612$$

16.
$$789 \times 876$$

17.
$$3428 \times 6123$$

18.
$$5967 \times 7298$$

19.
$$7642 \times 3850$$

20.
$$9743 \times 3006$$

21.
$$9537 \times 4060$$

Part 3: Division

(If necessary, round off all answers to two decimal places.)

1. $465 \div 15 =$ _____

2. $320 \div 16 =$ _____

3. $575 \div 25 =$ _____

4. $492 \div 12 =$ _____

5. $288 \div 24 =$ _____

6. $6095 \div 265 =$ _____

7. $4000 \div 125 =$ _____

8. $7231 \div 627 =$ _____

9. $4283 \div 252 =$ _____

10. $3985 \div 423 =$ _____

11. $4397 \div 2356 =$ _____

12. $9487 \div 8765 =$ _____

13. $5643 \div 1917 =$ _____

14. $1940 \div 1197 =$ _____

15. $7878 \div 3267 =$ _____

Part 4: Addition and Subtraction of Fractions

(Reduce all answers to lowest terms.)

1. $\frac{2}{3} + \frac{1}{2} + \frac{5}{6} =$ _____

2. $\frac{11}{16} + \frac{3}{4} + \frac{5}{8} =$ _____

3. $\frac{7}{8} + \frac{2}{3} + \frac{3}{4} =$ _____

4. $\frac{1}{3} + \frac{3}{8} + \frac{4}{7} =$ _____

5. $\frac{5}{6} + \frac{4}{9} + \frac{1}{4} =$ _____

6. $\frac{9}{16} + \frac{1}{2} + \frac{1}{3} =$ _____

7. $\frac{3}{4} - \frac{5}{9} =$ _____

8. $\frac{7}{10} - \frac{23}{45} =$ _____

9. $\frac{24}{71} - \frac{31}{213} =$ _____

10. $\frac{9}{10} - \frac{7}{15} =$ _____

11. $\frac{29}{54} - \frac{17}{36} =$ _____

12. $\frac{37}{49} - \frac{8}{14} =$ _____

Part 5: Conversions

Convert to decimals.

1. $\frac{5}{8} =$ _____

2. $\frac{9}{10} =$ _____

3. $\frac{12}{66} =$ _____

Convert to fractions.

4. $0.50 =$ _____

5. $0.75 =$ _____

6. $0.275 =$ _____

Find the following percentages.

7. 30% of 65 = _____

8. 25% of 400 = _____

9. 17% of 172 = _____

10. 88% of 990 = _____

11. 125% of 8 = _____

12. 93% of 422 = _____

13. What percent of 25 is 5? _____

14. What percent of 452 is 63.28? = _____

15. What percent of 320 is 96? _____

16. 91 is 28% of what number? _____

17. 60 is 40% of what number? _____

18. 2084.58 is 37% of what number? _____

Part 6: Proportion

Find the unknown quantities.

1. 2:4 = 6:_____

2. 7:9 = 21:_____

3. 3:6 = 5:_____

4. 2:_____ = 7:35

5. 10:6 = _____:18

6. _____:12 = 5:30

Part 7: Powers and Roots

Find the indicated powers.

1. 6^2 = _____

2. 14^3 = _____

3. 265^2 = _____

4. 12^3 = _____

5. 25^2 = _____

6. 100^4 = _____

Find the square root.

7. 1728 = _____

8. 15 129 = _____

9. 974 = _____

10. 1314.0625 = _____

11. 1339.78 = _____

12. 760.89 = _____

Part 8: Scientific Notation

Express the following in scientific notation with no more than one digit to the left of the decimal point.

1. 123 450 000 _____

2. 0.312 508 _____

3. 0.000 314 67 _____

4. 173 _____

5. 325 000 _____

6. 0.012 24 _____

Write the number indicated.

7. 8.42×10^9 _____

8. 1.226×10^2 _____

9. 3.674×10^{-4} _____

10. 1.344×10^{-1} _____

Part 9: Geometry/Trigonometry

1. Define an isosceles triangle.

_____

2. If the sum of two angles in a triangle is 120°, what is the value of the other angle?

_____

3. What is the length of the hypotenuse of a right triangle when the lengths of the other two sides are 6 in and 8 in?

_____

4. One side of a parallelogram is 8 in long and the perpendicular distance from this side to the opposite side is 5 in. What is the area of the parallelogram?

_____

5. The base of a triangle is 10 in and its height is 7 in. What is the area of the triangle?

_____

6. Give the area of a circle having a diameter of 9 in.

_____

7. If a rectangular fuel tank is 2 ft long, 18 in wide, and 8 in deep, what is its volume in cubic inches? If there are 231 in^3 in a gallon, how many gallons can the tank hold?

_____

8. If a 12-in sphere is submerged in a tank of water, how many gallons of water will it displace?

_____

9. What is the volume of a cone having a base with a 10-in diameter and an altitude of 12 in?

_____

In the following problems, the right angle will always be angle *C*. Angle *A* will be the smaller of the two acute angles, if they are not equal. Uppercase letters refer to angles and lowercase letters refer to sides.

10. *A* = 30, *a* = 1.8. Find *c*.

_____

11. *A* = 45, *b* = 3.5. Find *c*.

_____

12. *a* = 3, *b* = 4. Find *c*.

_____

13. What is the value of the sine of angle *B* in Problem 10?

_____

14. What is the value of the sine of 39°?

_____

15. What is the value of the cosine of 39°?

_____

Part 10: Charts

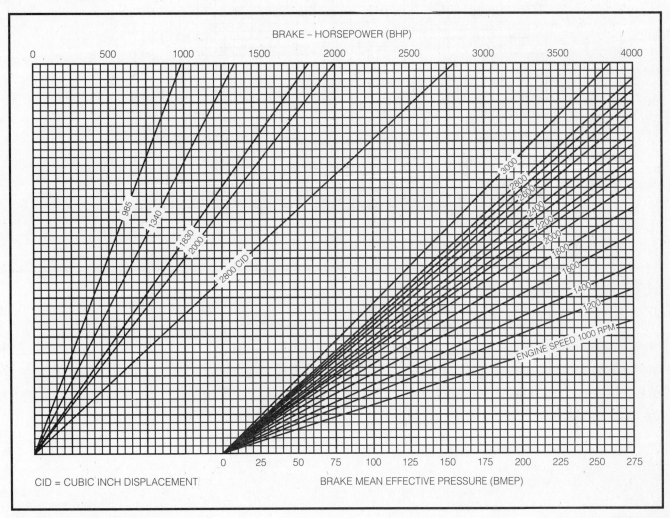

FIGURE 1–A Performance Chart

Using the example as a guide, find the specified information.

EXAMPLE: An aircraft engine has a 2800-in³ displacement and develops 2000 brake horsepower at 2200 rpm. What is the brake mean effective pressure?

To find the answer, first locate the point on Figure 1–A where the *2800 CID* line intersects with the vertical line representing *2000 BHP*. Move horizontally from this point until you intersect the *2200 rpm* line; from this point read the BMEP value from the bottom line of the chart.

Answer: 258 (approx.)

1. An aircraft reciprocating engine has a 1340-in³ displacement and develops a BMEP of 200 at 1800 rpm. What is the BHP?

   Answer: _____

2. An aircraft engine has a 2800-in³ displacement, develops 1800 brake horsepower, and indicates 250 brake mean effective pressure. What is the engine speed (rpm)?

   Answer: _____

3. An aircraft has a 2000-in³ displacement, and develops 1250 brake horsepower at 2000 rpm. What is the BMEP?

   Answer: _____

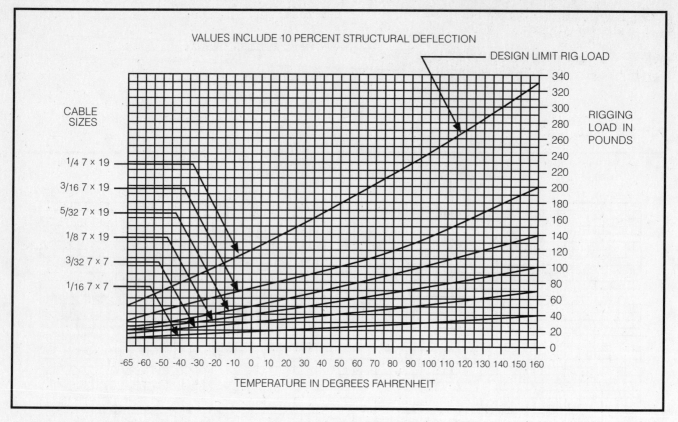

FIGURE 1–B Cable Tension Chart

Using Figure 1–B, determine the tension (rigging load) for the following cables:

4. $\frac{1}{8}$-in cable at 40°F _____

5. $\frac{1}{8}$-in cable at 70°F _____

6. $\frac{1}{16}$-in cable at 70°F _____

7. $\frac{1}{4}$-in cable at 50°F _____

8. $\frac{3}{16}$-in cable at 80°F _____

9. $\frac{3}{32}$-in cable at 60°F _____

10. $\frac{5}{32}$-in cable at 60°F _____

Chapter 1

REVIEW EXAM

Name _____

Date _____

Circle the letter of the best answer.

1. What power of 10 is equal to 1 000 000?
   a. 10 to the third power
   c. 10 to the fifth power
   b. 10 to the fourth power
   d. 10 to the sixth power

2. What is the square root of 4 raised to the fifth power?
   a. 32
   b. 64
   c. 16
   d. 20

3. What size sheet of metal is required to fabricate a cylinder 20 in long and 8 in in diameter? Note: $C = 3.1416 \times d$
   a. 20 in $\times 25\frac{5}{32}$
   c. 20 in $\times 25\frac{9}{64}$
   b. 20 in $\times 24\frac{9}{64}$
   d. 20 in $\times 24\frac{5}{32}$

4. Select the container size that will be equal in volume to 60 gal of fuel. (7.5 gal. = 1 ft^3)
   a. 7.0 ft^3
   c. 8.0 ft^3
   b. 7.5 ft^3
   d. 8.5 ft^3

5. Select the fraction that is equal to 0.020.
   a. $\frac{3}{16}$
   b. $\frac{1}{5}$
   c. $\frac{2}{7}$
   d. $\frac{1}{50}$

6. Select the decimal that is equal to the mixed number $1\frac{7}{32}$.
   a. 1.2188
   b. 1.3932
   c. 1.7320
   d. 1.3270

7. If the volume of a cylinder with the piston at bottom center is 84 in^3 and the piston displacement is 70 in^3, then the compression ratio is
   a. 7:1
   b. 1.2:1
   c. 6:1
   d. 1.9:1

8. What is the speed of a spur gear with 42 teeth driven by a pinion gear with 14 teeth turning at 420 rpm?
   a. 14 rpm
   c. 160 rpm
   b. 42 rpm
   d. 140 rpm

9. Select the fractional equivalent for a 0.09375-in thick sheet of aluminum.
   a. $\frac{5}{64}$
   b. $\frac{5}{32}$
   c. $\frac{3}{64}$
   d. $\frac{3}{32}$

10. An engine of 125 hp maximum is running at 65 percent power. What is the horsepower being developed?
    a. 93.05
    b. 30.85
    c. 81.25
    d. 38.85

Chapter 2

STUDY QUESTIONS

1. A system of measurement used widely throughout the world called the International System of Units, or SI, is commonly referred to as the _____.

2. Most airplane airspeed indicators are calibrated in _____.

3. The universal force that all bodies exert upon one another is called _____.

4. The pull exerted upon a body by the gravitation of the earth is _____.

5. The property of a body that is a measure of the amount of material it contains is _____.

6. A unit of mass having a value of approximately 32.175 lb under standard atmospheric conditions is a _____.

7. An important physical property of a substance is its mass per unit volume, which is referred to as its _____.

8. The ratio of the density of a substance to the density of water is called its _____.

9. A device used for measuring the specific gravity of liquids is called a _____.

10. A measure of how fast something is moving without respect to direction is its _____.

11. The rate at which an object's position changes over time and the direction of the change is its _____.

12. The tendency of matter to remain at rest if at rest, or to continue in motion in a straight line if in motion is defined as _____.

13. The rate at which velocity changes is _____.

14. The highest velocity that is reached by a falling object is called its _____ velocity.

15. The force that opposes motion between two surfaces that are touching is _____.

16. A reaction force that is measured in pounds is _____.

17. The two kinds of momentum are _____ and _____.

18. A weight attached to the end of a cord and twirled around will produce a force tending to cause the weight to fly outward called _____ force and an equal and opposite force pulling the weight inward called _____ force.

19. The product of the force applied to an object and the distance the object moves in the direction of the force is called _____.

20. The capacity for doing work is called _____.

21. There are two forms of energy: _____ energy and _____ energy.

22. The form of energy possessed by a body because of its position or configuration is called _____ energy.

23. The energy possessed by a body because of its motion is _____ energy.

24. The statement that "energy can be neither created nor destroyed; it can only be changed in form" is called the law of _____.

25. The number of times a machine increases the applied effort force is called the _____.

26. List four types of simple machines. _____ _____

_____ _____

27. Every lever has a _____, an _____ arm, and a

_____ arm.

28. A machine made by combining two or more simple machines is called a _____ machine.

29. As the heat of an object is increased, the motion of the molecules _____.

30. The degree of heat or cold (heat energy) measurable in a body is called _____.

31. Four different temperature scales that are used are _____, _____,

_____, and _____.

32. In the metric system the heat unit is called the _____.

33. In the English system the unit of heat measurement is called the _____.

34. A Btu is the amount of heat necessary to raise the temperature of _____ lb of water through _____° F.

35. The _____ heat of a substance is the number of calories required to raise the temperature of 1 g of the substance 1°C or the number of Btu's required to raise 1 lb of the substance 1°F.

36. The energy needed to change matter from the solid state to the liquid state or from a liquid to a solid is called the

heat of _____.

37. The energy involved in changing matter from a liquid to a gas, or from a gas to a liquid is called the heat

of _____.

38. There are three basic methods by which heat is transferred between locations and substances; they are

_____, _____, and _____.

39. Heat is transferred from the sun to the earth by _____.

40. _____ is the transfer of energy through a conductor by means of molecular activity and without any external motion.

41. _____ is the process by which heat is transferred through fluids by the movement of matter.

42. The resistance of a fluid to flow is called _____.

43. The pressure exerted at the bottom of a column of liquid is determined by the _____ of the

liquid and the _____ of the column.

44. The equation $F = P \times A$ represents _____ equals _____ times

_____.

45. The three states of matter are: _____, _____,

and _____.

46. Boyle's law states that the volume of a confined body of gas varies _____ as its absolute pressure, the temperature remaining constant.

47. Charles' law states that the volume of a gas varies in _____ to the absolute temperature.

48. The _____ law is derived by combining Boyle's law and Charles' law.

49. Sound is caused by the _____ of a substance.

50. The number of complete cycles occurring per second is the _____ of the vibration.

51. The unit for frequency is the _____.

52. The _____ of the vibration is the distance from the midpoint of the swing to the point of maximum displacement.

53. The distance of the vibrating point from the midpoint of vibration at any particular time is the

_____.

54. The two different kinds of wave motion are _____ and _____.

55. Sound intensity levels are measured by a unit called the _____.

Chapter 2

APPLICATION QUESTIONS

Name _____

Date _____

1. Convert the following temperatures:

   a. $110°F =$ _____ $°C$

   b. $35°C =$ _____ $°K$

   c. $200°F =$ _____ $°R$

   d. $1200°K =$ _____ $°C$

   e. $1850°R =$ _____ $°F$

   f. $90°C =$ _____ $°F$

2. Match the correct number with the appropriate description of the following levers.

   a. _____ First-class lever

   b. _____ Second-class lever

   c. _____ Third-class lever

   1.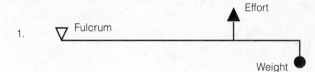

   2.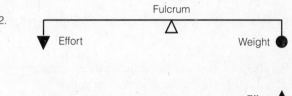

   3.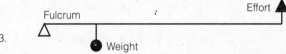

3. What does the distance D_1 need to be in order to balance the lever?

   _____ in

   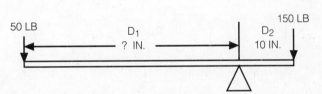

4. How many pounds of effort force needs to be applied at point A in order to lift the weight at point B?

   _____ lb

5. The amount of force applied to rope A to lift the weight is

_____ lb.

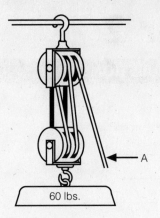

60 lbs.

6. An engine that weighs 350 lb is removed from an aircraft by means of a mobile hoist. The engine is raised 3 ft above its attachment mount, and the entire assembly is then moved forward 12 ft. A constant force of 70 lb is required to move the loaded hoist. What is the total work input required to move the hoist?

_____ ft-lb

7. What force must be applied to roll a 120-lb barrel up an inclined plane 9 ft long to a height of 3 ft (disregard friction)?

_____ lb

8. How much work input is required to lower (not drop) a 120-lb weight from the top of a 3-ft table to the floor?

_____ ft-lb

9. The force that can be produced by an actuating cylinder whose piston has a cross-sectional area of 3 in^2 operating in a 1000-psi hydraulic system is most nearly

_____ lb.

10. Solve the following fluid power problems.

a. Find P: Area = 4 in^2
               Force = 100 lb

               Pressure = _____ psi

b. Find A: Area = _____ in^2
               Force = 500 lb
               Pressure = 50 psi

c. Find F: Area = 10 in^2

               Force = _____ lb
               Pressure = 100 psi

d. Find P: Area = 3 in^2
               Force = 150 lb

               Pressure = _____ psi

e. Find A: Area = _____ in^2
               Force = 800 lb
               Pressure = 40 psi

f. Find F: Area = 2 in^2

               Force = _____ lb
               Pressure = 1000 psi

g. Find P: Area = 6 in^2
               Force = 150 lb

               Pressure = _____ psi

h. Find A: Area = _____ in^2
               Force = 750 lb
               Pressure = 100 psi

11. Match the following gas equations with their correct name.

a. _____ Charles' law

b. _____ General gas law

c. _____ Boyle's law

1. $\dfrac{V_1}{V_2} = \dfrac{P_2}{P_1}$

2. $\dfrac{V_1}{V_2} = \dfrac{T_1}{T_2}$

3. $\dfrac{P_1V_1}{T_1} = \dfrac{P_2V_2}{T_2}$

Chapter 2

Name _____

Date _____

Circle the letter of the best answer.

1. The amount of matter in a body is called its:
   a. volume   b. weight   c. mass   d. contents

2. The ratio of the density of a solid or a liquid to the density of pure water is called the
   _____ of the material.
   a. density ratio   c. specific density
   b. specific gravity   d. relative density

3. If the container volume of a confined gas is doubled (assume temperature remains constant), the pressure will
   a. increase in direct proportion to the volume increase.
   b. remain the same.
   c. be doubled.
   d. be reduced to one-half its original value.

4. If the temperature of a confined liquid is held constant and its pressure is tripled, its volume will
   a. triple.
   b. be increased by one-third its original volume.
   c. be reduced to one-third its original volume.
   d. remain the same.

5. If the fluid pressure is 800 psi in a 1/2-in line supplying an actuating cylinder with a piston area of 10 in^2, the force exerted on the piston will be
   a. 4000 lb.   c. 8000 lb.
   b. 1600 lb.   d. 800 lb.

6. How many of the following factors are necessary to determine power?

   Force exerted.
   Distance the force moves.
   Time required to do the work.

   a. None   c. Two
   b. One   d. Three

7. Which of the following is not considered a method of heat transfer?
   a. Convection   c. Diffusion
   b. Conduction   d. Radiation

8. One of the following equals 1 hp.
   a. 2000 ft-lb of work per minute
   b. 550 ft-lb of work per minute
   c. 2000 ft-lb of work per second
   d. 33 000 ft-lb of work per minute

9. If both the volume and the absolute temperature of a confined gas are doubled, the pressure will
   a. not change.
   b. be doubled.
   c. be halved.
   d. become four times as great.

10. A substance's mass per unit volume is its
    a. mass
    b. weight
    c. density
    d. specific gravity

11. The rate at which velocity changes is its
    a. speed   c. knots
    b. velocity   d. acceleration

12. The capacity for doing work is called
    a. centrifugal force   c. friction
    b. energy   d. thrust

13. The motion that opposes movement between two surfaces that are touching is called
    a. kinetic energy   c. viscosity
    b. momentum   d. friction

14. The energy involved in changing matter from a liquid to a gas is the heat of
    a. evaporation   c. energy
    b. fusion   d. temperature

15. Sound intensity levels are measured in
    a. frequency   c. amplitude
    b. hertz   d. decibels

Chapter 3

STUDY QUESTIONS

1. Pure dry air contains about 78 percent _____ and 21 percent _____.

2. Atmospheric pressure at sea level under standard conditions is _____ in of mercury, or _____ psi.

3. Under standard conditions, temperature decreases at approximately _____ for each 1000 ft of altitude.

4. Density varies _____ with pressure, with the temperature remaining constant.

5. The _____ is a unit of mass with a value of approximately 32.175 lb.

6. Air _____ decreases as you increase altitude.

7. On damp days air density is _____ than it is on dry days.

8. Bernoulli's principle states that as the air velocity increases, the pressure _____, and as the velocity decreases, the pressure _____.

9. The force created by increased air velocity over an airfoil, which causes a decrease in air pressure on the top of an airfoil, is called _____.

10. A surfaced body that responds to the relative motion between itself and the air with a useful dynamic reaction is called an _____.

11. The _____ is a straight line across the airfoil connecting the leading and trailing edges.

12. The curvature of an airfoil from the leading edge to the trailing edge is called the _____.

13. The distance between the upper and lower surface of an airfoil is called the _____.

14. The _____ flows opposite the flight direction of the airfoil.

15. The acute angle formed between the airfoil chord and the relative wind is the

_____.

16. The critical angle of attack is also referred to as the _____ angle.

17. Lift varies as the _____ of the speed.

18. Lift is _____ proportional to density.

19. Increasing the _____ of the wing causes the lift to increase.

20. The force that tends to retard or resist the motion of a body through the air is _____.

21. The frictional resistance that results when an object is moved through a viscous fluid is called

_____ drag.

22. The resistance of a fluid to flow is _____.

23. The _____ is the layer of air adjacent to the airfoil surface.

24. Airflow for numbers below the critical Reynolds number is _____, and is

_____ for numbers above the critical Reynolds number.

25. _____ drag is the resistance of the air produced by any part of the airplane that does not produce lift.

26. Drag caused by interfering airflows between intersecting parts is called
_____.

27. The drag that results during the production of lift is called _____ drag.

28. Total drag may be classified into two main types: _____ drag and
_____ drag.

29. The total aerodynamic force acting on the wing is called the _____.

30. The component of the resultant force that acts perpendicular to the relative wind is called
_____.

31. The component of the resultant force that acts parallel to the relative wind is called _____.

32. The _____ is the point at which the chord of an airfoil section
intersects the line of action of the resultant aerodynamic forces.

33. The center of pressure is generally located at the _____ percent chord position.

34. High-speed flight deals with air as though it is a _____ fluid.

35. The rate at which small pressure disturbances spread through the air is called the
_____.

36. The speed of sound varies with a change in the air _____.

37. The ratio of the speed of the aircraft to the speed of sound is referred to as the aircraft's
_____.

38. List the names of the regimes of flight associated with each of these speed ranges:

   a. Below Mach 0.75 _____

   b. Between Mach 0.75 and Mach 1.20 _____

   c. Between Mach 1.20 and Mach 5.00 _____

   d. Above Mach 5.00 _____

39. The flight Mach number at which there is the first indication of sonic flow is called the
_____.

40. Three fundamental types of waves formed in supersonic flight are the _____ shock wave, the
_____ shock wave, and the _____ wave.

41. The Mach number where shock wave airflow separation results in a rapid increase in the airfoil drag coefficient is
called the _____ Mach number.

42. Shock waves that extend to the ground and are reflected result in _____.

Chapter 3

APPLICATION QUESTIONS

1. Referring to Table 3-2 in the textbook, what is the speed of sound at the following altitudes?

   a. Sea level: _____ kn

   b. 10 000 ft: _____ kn

   c. 25 000 ft: _____ kn

   d. 40 000 ft: _____ kn

2. Match the statement with the proper word:

   a. _____ The layer of air adjacent to the airfoil surface.

   b. _____ The component of the resultant force that acts perpendicular to the relative wind.

   c. _____ That drag that is incurred by any portion of the aircraft that does not contribute directly to lift or thrust.

   d. _____ The frictional resistance incurred when an object is moved through a viscous fluid.

   e. _____ A surfaced body that responds to the relative motion between itself and the air with a useful dynamic reaction.

   f. _____ The drag that acts parallel to the relative wind and is the result of the production of lift.
   1. Airfoil
   2. Boundary layer
   3. Skin friction drag
   4. Parasite drag
   5. Induced drag
   6. Lift

3. In the following diagram, match the number with the correct definition.

   a. _____ Angle of attack

   b. _____ Lift

   c. _____ Drag

   d. _____ Center of pressure

   e. _____ Resultant

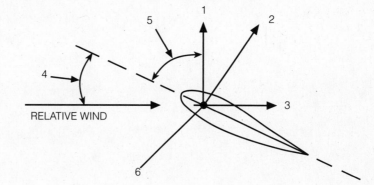

RELATIVE WIND

4. In the following diagram, match the number with the correct words.

a. _____ Chord

b. _____ Trailing edge

c. _____ Leading edge

d. _____ Camber

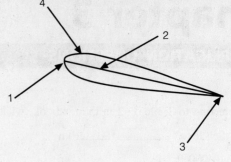

Chapter 3

Name _____

Date _____

Circle the letter of the best answer.

1. The density of the air is highest on
   a. warm dry days.
   b. cool dry days.
   c. warm wet days.
   d. cool wet days.

2. When the lift of an airfoil increases, the drag will
   a. decrease.
   b. not be affected.
   c. also increase.
   d. increase while the lift is changing but will return to its original value.

3. The drag that results from the production of lift is
   a. parasite drag.
   b. induced drag.
   c. profile drag.
   d. total drag.

4. A wing obtains most of its lift from which of the following?
   a. The increase in velocity of the air which flows under the wing
   b. The slower air moving above the wing exerting less downward pressure on it
   c. The impact pressure from the air striking the bottom of the wing
   d. The reduced pressure above the wing due to the increase in velocity of flow over the top surface

5. The critical Reynolds number is used to predict
   a. the amount of lift produced by an airfoil.
   b. the amount of drag produced by an airfoil.
   c. the point where airflow turns turbulent.
   d. the point where the boundary layer begins.

6. Lift varies
   a. directly with speed.
   b. inversely with speed.
   c. as the square of the speed.
   d. as the square root of the speed.

7. The resultant aerodynamic force on the airfoil
   a. intersects the chord of the wing at the center of pressure.
   b. intersects the chord of the wing at the center of gravity.
   c. acts perpendicular to the relative wind.
   d. is the resultant of the thrust and drag.

8. Bernoulli's theorem states
   a. the pressure of a fluid stream is least where the velocity is greatest, and the pressure is greatest where the velocity is least.
   b. the pressure of any fluid stream is least where the velocity is least, and the pressure is greatest where the velocity is greatest.
   c. the pressure of any fluid stream remains constant regardless of the velocity.
   d. pressure changes as the square of the velocity increases.

9. Generally, as altitude increases, temperature will
   a. remain constant.
   b. double every 10 000 ft.
   c. also increase.
   d. decrease.

10. The acute angle formed by the chord line of a wing and the relative wind is known as the
    a. longitudinal dihedral angle.
    b. angle of climb.
    c. angle of incidence.
    d. angle of attack.

11. Interference drag is reduced by
    a. fillets and fairings.
    b. high aspect ratio wings.
    c. smooth skin and streamline shapes.
    d. area rule.

12. The distance between the upper and lower surfaces on an airfoil is called the
    a. camber.
    b. thickness.
    c. mean line.
    d. chord.

13. Lift acts
    a. perpendicular to the chord of the wing.
    b. vertically through the centerline of the fuselage.
    c. perpendicular to the relative wind.
    d. perpendicular to the center of gravity.

14. Laminar flow is most likely to occur on an aircraft wing where the skin surface is
    a. rough.
    b. convex.
    c. smooth.
    d. cambered.

15. The center of pressure is also referred to as the
    a. resultant.
    b. mean aerodynamic chord.
    c. angle of attack.
    d. center of lift.

16. The chord of a wing is measured from
    a. wingtip to wingtip.
    b. wing attachment point to the wingtip.
    c. leading edge to trailing edge.
    d. maximum upper camber to the base line.

17. The net result of lift and drag vectors is
    a. relative wind.
    b. center of pressure.
    c. the resultant force.
    d. coefficient of lift.

18. Lift varies
    a. inversely with area.
    b. as the square of the speed.
    c. inversely with density.
    d. All of the above

19. The curvature of the wing surface is called
    a. sweepback.
    b. dihedral.
    c. camber.
    d. taper.

20. A stall is the direct result of
    a. uncoordinated control use.
    b. excessive angle of attack.
    c. decreased load attack.
    d. skidding turn.

21. Supersonic airflow passing through a constriction
    would be characterized by
    a. increasing velocity, decreasing pressure,
       decreasing density.
    b. decreasing velocity, increasing pressure,
       increasing density.
    c. increasing velocity, decreasing pressure, constant
       density.
    d. decreasing velocity, increasing pressure, constant
       density.

22. The speed of sound is
    a. the speed when the first airflow on an aircraft
       goes supersonic.
    b. the ratio of the aircraft speed to the temperature.
    c. the speed of the relative wind.
    d. the rate at which pressure disturbances will spread
       through the air.

23. As the speed of sound increases
    a. temperature decreases.
    b. temperature increases.
    c. humidity increases.
    d. humidity decreases.

24. The speed of the aircraft in relation to the speed of
    sound is called
    a. Mach number.
    b. local speed.
    c. sound barrier.
    d. critical Mach number.

25. The critical Mach number of any airplane is reached
    a. when the airplane is at Mach 0.75.
    b. when any of the local flows around the wing
       reach the speed of sound.
    c. when the airplane is at Mach 1.
    d. more easily at low altitudes.

Chapter 4

1. An _____ is any surface, such as an airplane wing, aileron, or rudder, designed to obtain reaction from the air through which it moves.

2. An _____ is the outline of an airfoil section.

3. An _____ is a cross section of an airfoil parallel to the plane of symmetry or to a specified reference plane.

4. The following letters are used in airfoil designation. List the correct meaning for each abbreviation.

   NACA _____

   NASA _____

   GAW _____

5. NACA and NASA numbers give information only on the _____ of the airfoil, not the size.

6. Airfoil features that are collectively known as airfoil characteristics are classified as follows:

   a. _____

   b. _____

   c. _____

   d. _____

7. The _____ is a measure of how efficiently the wing is changing velocity into lift.

8. The _____ is the ratio of the lift to the drag of any body in flight and is a measure of the effectiveness of an airfoil.

9. The _____ is the ratio of the distance of the CP from the leading edge to the chord length.

10. _____ are graphical representations of airfoil characteristics for various angles of attack.

11. The _____ is a measure of the total surface of the wing.

12. The _____ of an airfoil of rectangular shape is the ratio of the span to the chord.

13. The effect of increasing the aspect ratio is principally to reduce _____ drag.

14. An airfoil is _____ when one or more of its dimensions gradually decreases from the root to the tip.

15. When the airfoil decreases from the root to the tip in both thickness and chord, the airfoil is said to have taper in _____ and _____.

16. The _____ is the ratio of the tip chord to the root chord.

17. The principal reason for sweeping a wing is to increase the _____ of the aircraft.

18. The _____ is the chord drawn through the center of area of the airfoil.

19. A _____ is a hinged, pivoted, or sliding airfoil, usually near the trailing edge of the wing.

20. The deflection of a flap produces the effect of adding a large amount of _____ well aft on the chord.

21. A _____ is a nozzle-shaped passage through a wing designed to improve the airflow conditions at high angles of attack and slow speeds.

22. A _____ is a movable auxiliary airfoil attached to the leading edge of the wing, which, when closed, falls within the original contour of the wing and which, when opened, forms a slot.

23. A device designed to reduce the lift on a wing is called a _____.

24. The _____ of a wing is the angle formed by the intersection of the wing chord line and the horizontal plane passing through the longitudinal axis of the aircraft.

25. Many airplanes are designed with a greater angle of incidence at the root of the wing than at the tip; this characteristic of a wing is called _____.

26. _____ is an increase in the angle of incidence of the wing from the root to the tip.

27. A _____ is a triangular strip mounted on the leading edge of the wing for the purpose of disrupting the airflow at high angles of attack.

28. In order to reduce the drag caused by supersonic flow over portions of the wing, small airfoils called _____ are installed vertically into the airstream.

29. A _____ is a stationary vane, projecting from the upper surface of an airfoil, which is used to prevent the spanwise flow of air.

30. The supercritical airfoil design prevents the rapid pressure rise normally associated with a more cambered airfoil and in turn delays and softens the onset of _____ on the upper surface of a wing.

Chapter 4

Name _____

Date _____

APPLICATION QUESTIONS

1. In the following diagram, match the number with the correct definition.

   a. _____ Taper in planform and thickness

   b. _____ Taper in thickness

   c. _____ Taper in planform

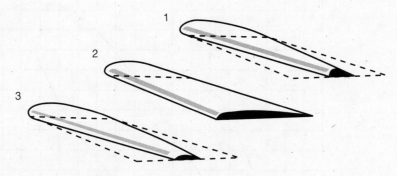

2. In the following diagram, match the number with the correct definition.

   a. _____ Split flap

   b. _____ Slotted flap

   c. _____ Fowler flap

   d. _____ Basic airfoil

   e. _____ Plain flap

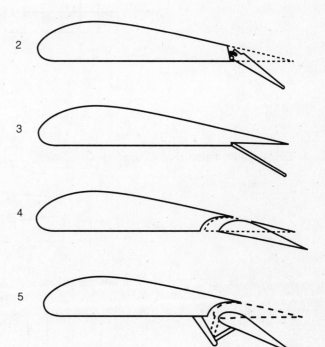

3. In the following diagram, match the number with the correct definition.

a. _____ Drag curve

b. _____ Lift curve

c. _____ Lift/drag curve

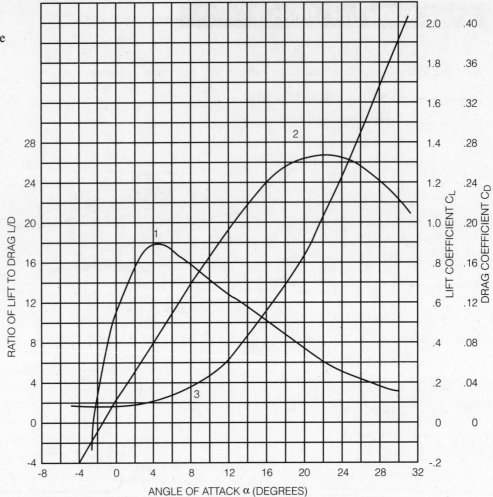

ANGLE OF ATTACK α (DEGREES)

4. Calculate the aspect ratio of the following airfoil. _____
   $b = 26.5$ ft
   $c = 7.5$ ft

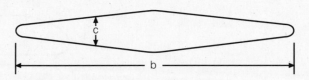

5. Calculate the taper ratio of the following airfoil. _____
   $C_R = 8$ ft
   $C_t = 2.5$ ft

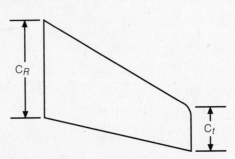

6. Calculate the lift for the following airfoil. _____

   Given: A/C speed = 190 mph
   A/C altitude = 4000 ft
   A/C wing area = 210 ft^2
   C_L = 0.08° 10 AOA

7. Calculate the drag for the following airfoil.

   Given: A/C speed = 170 kn
   A/C altitude = 9000 ft
   A/C wing area = 175 ft^2
   C_D = 0.6° 8 AOA

   NOTE: The speed in this problem is given in knots, *not* mph.

8. Calculate the lift/drag ratio for 10° AOA utilizing the lift and drag curves shown in Figure 4–10. _____

Chapter 4

REVIEW EXAM

Name _____

Date _____

Circle the letter of the best answer.

1. Flaps increase the effective lift of an airfoil by
   a. increasing the camber of the airfoil.
   b. introducing drag aft of the center of pressure.
   c. reducing the profile drag.
   d. reducing the induced drag.

2. The angle formed by the intersection of the wing chord line and the horizontal plane passing through the longitudinal axis of the aircraft is known as the
   a. longitudinal dihedral angle.
   b. angle of climb.
   c. angle of incidence.
   d. angle of attack.

3. Select the answer that properly describes the chart below.

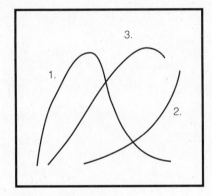

   a. 1. L/D 2. C_L 3. C_D
   b. 1. C_L 2. C_D 3. L/D
   c. 1. C_D 2. L/C 3. C_L
   d. 1. L/D 2. C_D 3. C_L

4. NASA and NACA numbers are used to describe
   a. the date an airfoil was tested.
   b. the shape of an airfoil profile.
   c. the size of an airfoil profile.
   d. the shape and size of an airfoil profile.

5. A form of drag that is the result of the wing tip vortices is
   a. parasitic.   c. interference.
   b. induced.   d. friction.

6. When spoilers are deployed on a wing they act to _____ lift.
   a. increase   c. decrease
   b. stabilize   d. multiply

7. Induced drag may be reduced by
   a. decreasing the fineness ratio.
   b. increasing the aspect ratio.
   c. decreasing the aspect ratio.
   d. adding fillets or fairings to smooth out flow.

8. The MAC is
   a. the chord drawn through the center of an area.
   b. the average geometric chord.
   c. parallel to the center of pressure.
   d. the same as the average chord.

9. What physical factors are involved in the aspect ratio of airplane wings?
   a. Thickness and chord
   b. Span and chord
   c. Dihedral and angle of attack
   d. Sweepback and lateral axis

10. Sweeping a wing back will
    a. increase lift at low speeds.
    b. increase the critical Mach number.
    c. decrease the critical Mach number.
    d. have no effect on the critical Mach number.

11. The angle of incidence of an airplane
    a. is changed by the pilot while climbing.
    b. affects the dihedral of the wings.
    c. is the angle between the relative wind and the chord of the wing.
    d. does not change in flight.

12. The primary purpose of stall strips is to
    a. provide added lift at slow speeds.
    b. stall the inboard portions of the wing first.
    c. provide lateral stability at cruise speed and above.
    d. provide added lift at high angles of attack.

13. Vortex generators are designed to
    a. provide emergency power in the event of alternator failure.
    b. help keep the airflow over the wing attached at higher angles of attack.
    c. increase the airfoil stall speed.
    d. increase vertical stability.

14. A wing slat is a movable airfoil attached to the leading edge of a high-performance airplane wing. Its purpose is to
   a. reduce stalling speed.
   b. replace flaps.
   c. act as a dive brake or speed brake.
   d. increase speed on takeoff.

15. A wing with a greater angle of incidence at the root than at the tip is said to
   a. be washed in.
   b. be washed out.
   c. have a high dihedral angle.
   d. have a negative angle of attack.

Chapter 5

STUDY QUESTIONS

1. The four forces acting on an airplane in flight are _____, _____, _____, and _____.

2. Weight acts vertically downward from the _____.

3. Lift acts in a direction perpendicular to the direction of the relative wind from the _____.

4. In straight and level flight the lift and _____ must be equal.

5. When the airplane is flying at a constant speed, the thrust must equal the _____.

6. The ratio of the total load supported by the airplane's wing to the actual weight of the airplane and its contents is referred to as the _____.

7. Aircraft may be type-certificated into _____, _____, or _____ categories.

8. The ratio of the total gross weight of the aircraft divided by the total wing area is called _____.

9. The inherent ability of a body, after its equilibrium is disturbed, to develop forces or moments that tend to return the body to its original position is called _____.

10. The initial tendency of an aircraft to return to equilibrium conditions following some disturbance from equilibrium is called _____.

11. If an object is disturbed from equilibrium and has the tendency to return to equilibrium, _____ static stability exists.

12. The property that dampens the oscillations set up by a statically stable airplane, enabling the oscillations to become smaller and smaller in magnitude until the airplane eventually settles down to its original condition of flight, is called _____.

13. While being supported in flight by lift, and propelled through the air by thrust, an airplane is free to revolve or move around three axes, namely the _____ axis, the _____ axis, and the _____ axis.

14. The axis that extends lengthwise through the fuselage from the nose to the tail is the _____ axis.

15. The axis extending through the fuselage from wing tip to wing tip is the _____ axis.

16. The axis that passes vertically through the fuselage at the center of gravity is the _____ axis.

17. The ailerons control _____ about the longitudinal axis, the elevators control _____ about the lateral axis, and the rudder controls _____ about the vertical axis.

18. The stability of an airplane about the lateral axis is _____ stability.

19. _____ stability is the stability of an airplane about the longitudinal or roll axis.

20. The factors that primarily affect lateral stability are _____ and _____.

21. The lateral angle of the wing with respect to a horizontal plane is called _____.

22. The stability of an airplane about the vertical axis is called _____ stability.

23. Directional stability is accomplished by placing a _____ to the rear of the center of gravity on the upper portion of the tail section.

24. The ability of an airplane to be directed along a selected flight path is called _____.

25. The fixed airfoils on an aircraft are the _____, the _____ stabilizer, and the _____ stabilizer.

26. The tail section of the airplane, including the stabilizers, elevators, and rudder, is commonly called the

_____.

27. The primary control surfaces of an airplane include the _____, _____, and _____.

28. Secondary control surfaces include _____, _____, _____, and _____.

29. The primary flight control surfaces utilized to provide lateral (roll) control of the aircraft are

_____.

30. The _____ is a vertical control surface that is usually hinged to the tail post aft of the vertical stabilizer and designed to apply yawing moments to the airplane.

31. The control surfaces that govern the movement of the aircraft around the lateral axis are the

_____.

32. A special type of elevator that combines the functions of the elevator and the horizontal stabilizer is called a _____.

33. Small secondary flight control surfaces set into the trailing edges of the primary control surfaces are called

_____.

34. Trim tabs that can be adjusted from the cockpit by means of control wheels, knobs, or cranks are called _____ trim tabs.

35. Tabs that are used primarily on the large main control surfaces that are directly operated by the primary controls of the airplane are called _____ tabs.

36. In a canard-equipped aircraft, the forward wing must always stall at a _____ angle of attack than the aft wing.

37. The distance between the leading edges of the upper and lower wings of a biplane is called the

_____.

38. The difference in the longitudinal position of the axes of two wings of a biplane is called

_____.

39. The difference between the angles of incidence of the wings of a biplane is called _____.

40. On a biplane during flight, the _____ wires are under a high-tension stress.

41. Before a helicopter takes off and when the rotor is turning in the horizontal position, _____ force is the main force acting on the rotor blades.

42. As the blade pitch is increased and power is applied to the rotor the lift force of the blades causes the blade tips to rise above the horizontal plane in an effect that is referred to as blade _____.

43. The difference in airspeed of the advancing and retreating rotor blades on a helicopter is referred to

    as _____.

44. Dissymmetry of lift is compensated for by the design of the rotor, which permits

    _____.

45. The flapping of rotor blades produces what is known as the _____,
    which occurs as the center of mass of the rotor moves closer to the center of rotation when the blades rise.

46. The result of Coriolis effect on a rotor is that the advancing blade moves _____ and the

    retreating blade moves _____ in respect to the blade attach point.

47. The leading and lagging of rotor blades is commonly referred to as blade _____.

48. The inherent quality of rotating bodies in which an applied force is manifested 90° in the direction of rotation from

    the point where the force is applied is called _____.

49. Rotor blade stall begins at the tip of the _____ blade and works inward as forward speed
    increases.

50. When a helicopter is moving horizontally in flight at more than 15 kn [7.7 m/s], the performance of the main rotor

    improves due to an effect called _____.

51. The torque force applied to the rotor shaft of a helicopter to turn the rotor will turn the fuselage of the helicopter in

    the _____ direction, unless measures are taken to prevent it.

52. The _____ control increases or decreases the pitch of all the
    main-rotor blades simultaneously or collectively.

53. The _____ control causes a variation of the blade pitch as each
    blade rotates through the tip-path plane.

54. The purpose of the cyclic-pitch control is to cause the _____
    of the main rotor to tilt as required to provide for movement of the helicopter in a desired direction.

55. The tail rotor is often called an _____ rotor.

56. The heading control for a helicopter is generally the _____.

57. During autorotation, _____ force, not engine force, is driving the rotor.

58. The phenomenon of self-excited vibrations that can cause the helicopter to rock fore-and-aft or sideways with

    increasing magnitude is known as _____.

Chapter 5

APPLICATION QUESTIONS

1. In the following diagram representing the four forces acting on an aircraft, match the number with the correct word.

   a. _____ Lift

   b. _____ Weight

   c. _____ Thrust

   d. _____ Drag

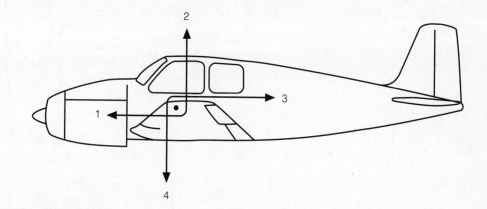

2. In the following diagram representing the three axes of movement of an aircraft, label the drawing with the correct axis, the resulting movement, and the responsible control surface.

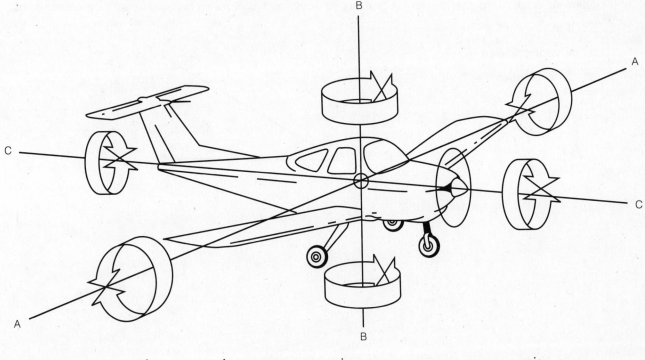

   a. _____ axis   b. _____ axis   c. _____ axis

   Movement: _____   Movement: _____   Movement: _____

   Controlled by _____   Controlled by _____   Controlled by _____

3. In the following diagram representing the control surfaces of an aircraft, match the number with the correct word.

a. _____ Rudder

b. _____ Elevators

c. _____ Vertical fin

d. _____ Horizontal stabilizer

e. _____ Flaps

f. _____ Ailerons

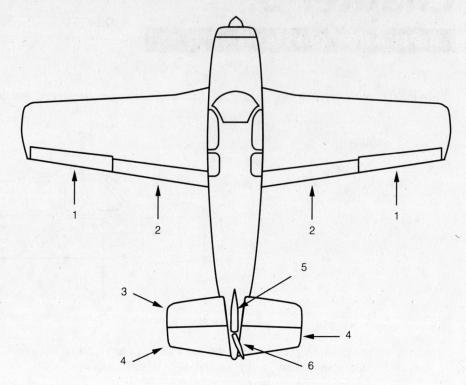

4. In the following diagram representing the forces acting on a rotating blade, match the number with the correct word.

a. _____ Lift

b. _____ Centrifugal force

c. _____ Blade position

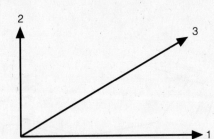

Chapter 5

REVIEW EXAM

Name _____

Date _____

Circle the letter of the best answer.

1. Motion about the lateral axis is called
   a. pitch.
   b. roll.
   c. yaw.
   d. horizontal.

2. In straight and level unaccelerated flight, which of the following is correct?
   a. Lift equals weight.
   b. Lift is greater than weight.
   c. Thrust is greater than drag.
   d. Thrust is less than drag.

3. Dihedral contributes most to stability of the airplane about its
   a. longitudinal axis.
   b. vertical axis.
   c. lateral axis.
   d. transverse axis.

4. If an aircraft has neutral static stability and is deflected from the attitude for which it is trimmed, it will
   a. return to its trimmed attitude.
   b. move further away from the trimmed attitude.
   c. remain in the new attitude.
   d. None of the above

5. When an aircraft has differential ailerons
   a. the down aileron deflects more than the up aileron.
   b. the up aileron deflects more than the down aileron.
   c. the ailerons move the same.
   d. the ailerons are tied to the rudders.

6. An aircraft with positive dynamic pitch stability
   a. would return to level flight directly after being displaced by an air gust.
   b. would return to level flight through a series of constantly reducing oscillations after being displaced by an air gust.
   c. would remain in a displaced attitude after being displaced by an air gust.
   d. would continue in the direction that it was displaced by an air gust.

7. Primary control surfaces on conventional aircraft are the
   a. ailerons, rudder trim, and elevators.
   b. elevator trim, ailerons, and rudder.
   c. ailerons, elevators, rudder.
   d. trim tabs, ailerons, elevators, rudder.

8. The ratio of the total gross weight of the aircraft divided by the total wing area is called
   a. load factor.
   b. gross weight.
   c. wing loading.
   d. G force.

9. The elevators of a conventional airplane are used to provide rotation about the
   a. longitudinal axis.
   b. lateral axis.
   c. directional axis.
   d. vertical axis.

10. The two forces acting along an aircraft's longitudinal axis are
    a. lift and gravity.
    b. lift and weight.
    c. thrust and weight.
    d. thrust and drag.

11. When the control wheel is displaced on the right
    a. the right aileron will move down.
    b. the right aileron will move up.
    c. the right elevator will move down.
    d. the right elevator will move up.

12. The purpose of spring tabs or servo tabs is to
    a. assist the pilot in moving the control surfaces.
    b. contribute to the static balance of the control surface.
    c. balance the weight of that portion of the control surface located aft of the hinge line.
    d. make in-flight trim adjustments possible.

13. If the control stick of an aircraft with properly rigged flight controls is moved rearward and to the left, the right aileron will move
    a. down and the elevator will move down.
    b. up and the elevator will move down.
    c. up and the elevator will move up.
    d. down and the elevator will move up.

14. The vertical flight of a helicopter is controlled by
    a. increasing or decreasing collective pitch.
    b. tilting the rotor disk.
    c. cyclic pitch changes.
    d. increasing or decreasing the rpm of the main rotor.

15. An airplane that has a tendency to gradually increase a pitching moment that has been set into motion has
    a. poor longitudinal stability.
    b. good lateral stability.
    c. poor lateral stability.
    d. good longitudinal stability.

16. Which statement is correct concerning torque effect on helicopters?
    a. As horsepower increases, torque decreases.
    b. Torque direction is the same as rotor blade rotation.
    c. As horsepower decreases, torque increases.
    d. Torque direction is the opposite of rotor blade rotation.

17. If the control stick of an aircraft with properly rigged flight controls is moved forward and to the right, the left aileron will move
    a. up and the elevator will move down.
    b. up and the elevator will move up.
    c. down and the elevator will move up.
    d. down and the elevator will move down.

18. Movement of an airplane along its lateral axis (roll) is also movement
    a. around or about the vertical axis controlled by the rudder.
    b. around or about the longitudinal axis controlled by the elevator.
    c. around or about the lateral axis controlled by the ailerons.
    d. around or about the longitudinal axis controlled by the ailerons.

19. Movement about the longitudinal (roll) in a helicopter is effected by movement of
    a. the drag hinge damper control.
    b. the collective pitch control.
    c. the cyclic pitch control.
    d. the tail rotor pitch control.

20. Movement about the lateral axis (pitch) in a helicopter is effected by movement of
    a. the drag hinge damper control.
    b. the collective pitch control.
    c. the cyclic pitch control.
    d. the tail rotor pitch control.

21. An airplane is controlled directionally about its vertical axis by
    a. the rudder.
    b. the elevator(s).
    c. the ailerons.
    d. a combination of two of the above.

22. The elevators of a conventional airplane are used to provide rotation about the
    a. longitudinal axis.
    b. lateral axis.
    c. directional axis.
    d. vertical axis.

23. A helicopter in forward flight, cruise configuration, changes direction of flight by
    a. varying the pitch of the main rotor blades equally.
    b. changing tail rotor rpm.
    c. tilting the main rotor disk in the desired direction.
    d. tilting the tail rotor.

24. Tilting of the rotor tip-path plane is controlled by the
    a. cyclic.
    b. collective.
    c. rudder pedals.
    d. throttle.

25. A tandem-rotor helicopter uses
    a. one main rotor and one tail rotor.
    b. two main rotors, counterrotating.
    c. two main rotors, same rotation direction.
    d. two main rotors, one tail rotor.

26. A decrease in the pitch of the tail rotor blades causes the fuselage of the ship to
    a. turn in the direction of the main rotor.
    b. turn in the opposite direction of the main rotor.
    c. ascend.
    d. descend.

27. What is the cause of main rotor-blade ''coning''?
    a. Centrifugal force
    b. Torque effect
    c. Lift force
    d. Coriolis effect

28. A single-rotor helicopter wishing to move toward the 6:00 position would need the highest blade pitch imputed at the
    a. 12:00 position.
    b. 3:00 position.
    c. 6:00 position.
    d. 9:00 position.

29. Gyroscopic precession causes the resultant ultimate force to occur how many degrees from the applied force?
    a. 90° in opposite direction of rotation.
    b. 90° in direction of rotation.
    c. 180° in opposite direction of rotation.
    d. 180° in direction of rotation.

30. Translational lift affects a helicopter that is
    a. moving horizontally at more than 15 kn.
    b. hovering.
    c. equipped with a tail rotor.
    d. All of the above

31. The difference between the angles of incidence for two airfoils on a biplane is called
    a. decalage.
    b. stagger.
    c. dihedral.
    d. gap.

32. The action of the rotor blade that minimizes the effects caused by dissymmetry of lift is
    a. flapping.
    b. hunting.
    c. twisting.
    d. advancing.

33. The principle factor in limiting helicopter maximum speed in forward flight is
    a. dissymmetry of lift.
    b. torque effect.
    c. advancing blade stall.
    d. retreating blade stall.

34. When the helicopter blades are at their lowest pitch and all have the same angle, the collective stick is
    a. centered and the cyclic stick is centered.
    b. full up and the cyclic stick is centered.
    c. centered and the cyclic stick is full aft.
    d. full down and the cyclic stick is centered.

35. What turns the main rotor during autorotation?
    a. The engine
    b. Aerodynamic forces
    c. A downward inflow of air
    d. A gigantic recirculation of air

36. The fastest moving point on a rotor blade is the
    a. advancing blade tip.
    b. advancing blade root.
    c. retreating blade tip.
    d. retreating blade root.

37. How is the torque force associated with single-rotor helicopters compensated?
    a. A tail rotor with a variable pitch mechanism
    b. A twist in the main rotor blade chord
    c. A vertical flat plate that is acted upon by the main rotor downwash
    d. A double set of planetary gears in the main transmission

38. In a hover, which component(s) act vertically?
    a. Lift
    b. Drag
    c. Thrust
    d. All of the above

39. Blade hunting is caused by
    a. gyroscopic precession.
    b. ground effect.
    c. transitional lift.
    d. coriolis effect.

40. The direction that a helicopter is facing may be changed by the
    a. collective control.
    b. cyclic control.
    c. antitorque pedals.
    d. All of the above

41. The tendency of a helicopter to drift in the direction of the tail rotor thrust is referred to as
    a. gyroscopic precession.
    b. ground effect.
    c. translational lift.
    d. translating tendency.

42. Rotor droop is counteracted by
    a. centrifugal force.
    b. thrust.
    c. ground effect.
    d. translational lift.

Chapter 6

STUDY QUESTIONS

1. Drawings used for the fabrication or assembly of components are called _____ or _____ drawings.

2. Production drawings can be categorized as _____, _____, or _____ drawings.

3. A _____ drawing will provide all specifications (size, shape, and material) needed to make the part.

4. An _____ drawing shows how parts fit together to form a component.

5. A _____ drawing is similar to a _____ and shows the parts as they would appear to the eye.

6. An _____ drawing shows how a part or component is installed in the aircraft.

7. A _____ diagram is a drawing used to simplify the explanation of complex circuits.

8. A _____ diagram shows the _____ location of components within a system without regard to the _____ location of the components in the aircraft.

9. A _____ diagram shows all the wires, wire segments, and connections in an electrical system or circuit.

10. Because of the complexity of electronic systems and the use of _____ systems involving solid-state electronic units, it has been necessary to simplify system drawings using _____ that have meaning to the electronic technician.

11. In a _____ drawing parallel lines will be shown as _____, which produces an effect known as foreshortening.

12. The _____ view is similar to the perspective, but the lines are drawn _____ and the _____ of each line is true to scale.

13. An _____ projection shows equal distances on the subject as equal distances on the drawing.

14. With isometric projection, all vertical lines are drawn as _____ and all horizontal lines are drawn at an angle of _____ degrees.

15. The three views most commonly used for orthographic projection are the _____, _____, and _____ side views.

16. Most drawings use three widths, or intensities, of lines: _____, _____, and _____.

17. The visible outline (object line) is a _____ to _____ line and should be the outstanding feature of the drawing.

18. The _____ outline is a medium-width line made up of short dashes.

19. The _____ line is drawn narrow, or thin, and consists of alternate long and short dashes.

20. The _____ line is used to show alternate positions for an installed part.

21. The dimension line is a _____ line and is unbroken except where a _____ is written in.

22. The _____ line is a heavy, wide, broken line usually made up of _____ long and _____ short dashes, alternately spaced.

23. When a surface has been cut away to reveal a hidden or inner feature of an object, _____ lines are used.

24. A curved surface or a circle appears in that form in only one view. In other views, the curve or the circle is shown as a _____ line.

25. A _____ view is obtained by cutting away part of an object to show the shape or construction at the _____ plane.

26. A _____ view shows only a portion of the object but in greater _____ than the principal view.

27. _____ are required on any drawing used to fabricate or repair parts.

28. When locating holes for drilling, the technician uses _____ dimensions.

29. When cutting a piece of stock to the size and shape for a part, _____ dimensions are used.

30. Dimensions common to two views are usually placed _____ the views.

31. Holes to be drilled in a part are located by dimensions to the _____.

32. A hole will often be dimensioned by the _____ of the _____ to be used.

33. Curved surfaces are often dimensioned as a _____ from a specified point. The dimension would be shown with a view that shows the curve as an _____.

34. The dimensions on a drawing that represent the nominal size are sometimes called the _____ dimensions.

35. All basic dimensions will have _____, or applicable _____ and _____ sizes.

36. The _____ is the total permissable variation of a size.

37. An _____ is a prescribed difference between the maximum material limits of _____.

38. The _____ is usually printed in large numerals in the lower right-hand corner of the title block.

39. Each part of an aerospace vehicle always has a _____ of its own.

40. An aircraft has many mirror image parts. To reduce the amount of paperwork it is common practice to show the part for one side in the drawing and indicate the other side as _____.

41. A _____ system can be used to help find the location of fuselage frames, wing frames, and stabilizer frames.

42. Information that cannot be given completely and yet briefly in the title block is placed on the drawing in the form of _____, but does not _____ information given elsewhere in the same drawing.

43. A _____ is a visible sign used instead of words to represent ideas, operations, quantities, qualities, relations, or positions.

44. To simplify changes, the symbol for _____ is often used to refer to all metals.

Chapter 6

Name _____

Date _____

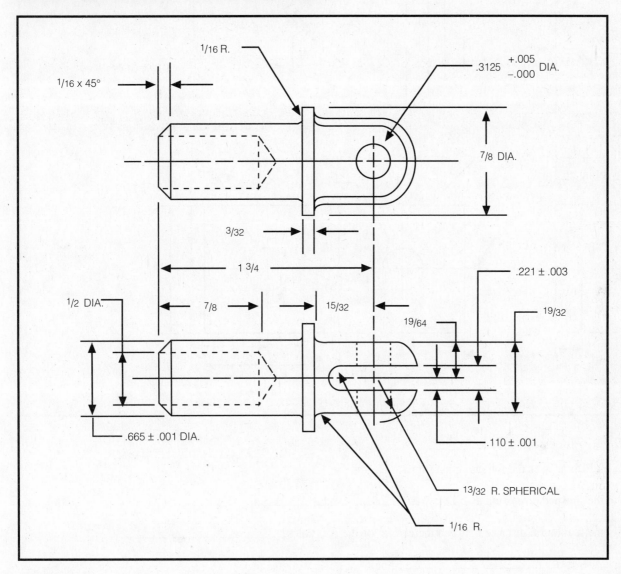

FIGURE 6–A

Use Figure 6–A to answer the following questions.

1. What is the minimum length of stock needed to make the pin? _____

2. What is the minimum diameter of the stock to make the pin? _____

3. What is the distance from the end of the pin to the center of the hole? _____

4. What is the minimum diameter allowed for the shank? _____

5. What is the maximum size of the hole in the head? _____

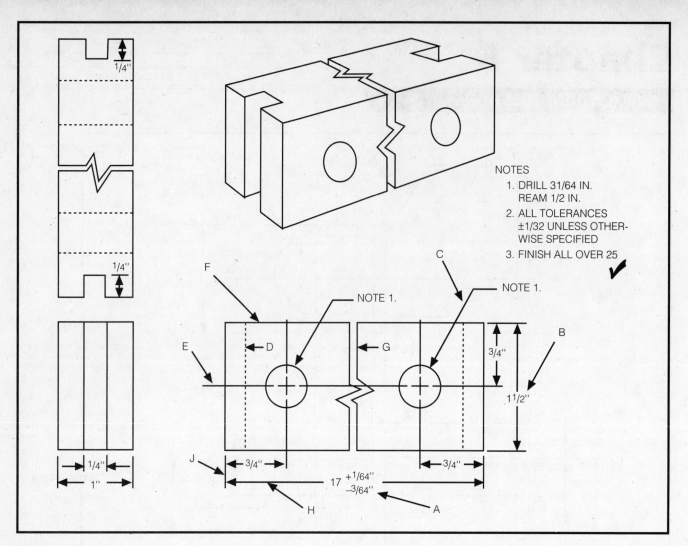

FIGURE 6–B

Use Figure 6–B to answer the following questions.

6. What is the finished size of the two holes? _____

7. What is the maximum distance between the centers of the two holes? _____

8. The line at *E* is a _____ line.

9. Line *J* is a _____ line.

10. The view in the upper right corner is a _____ view.

Chapter 6

Name _____

Date _____

Circle the letter of the best answer.

1. What type of line is normally used in mechanical drawing or blueprints to represent an edge or object not visible to the viewer?
   a. Medium-weight dashed line.
   b. Light solid line.
   c. Alternate short and long heavy dashes.
   d. Zigzag or wavy line.

2. (1) A detail drawing is a description of a single part.
   (2) An assembly drawing is a description of an object made up of two or more parts.
   Regarding the above statements,
   a. only No. 1 is true.
   b. only No. 2 is true.
   c. neither No. 1 nor No. 2 is true.
   d. both No. 1 and No. 2 are true.

3. Which statement is true regarding an orthographic projection?
   a. There are always at least two views.
   b. It could have as many as eight views.
   c. It must be accompanied by a pictorial drawing.
   d. One-view, two-view, and three-view drawings are the most common.

4. A line used to show an edge that is not visible is a
   a. position line.   c. hidden line.
   b. phantom line.   d. break line.

5. What are the means of conveying measurements through the medium of drawings?
   a. Dimensions   c. Edge distances
   b. Tolerances   d. Bend allowances

6. What is the allowable manufacturing tolerance for a bushing where the outside dimensions shown on the blueprint are: $1.0625 + 0.0025 - 0.0003$?
   a. 0.0028.   b. 1.0650.   c. 1.0647.   d. 0.0025.

7. The drawings often used in illustrated parts manuals are
   a. exploded-view drawings.
   b. block drawings.
   c. section drawings.
   d. detail drawings.

8. A drawing in which all of the parts are brought together as an assembly is called
   a. a sectional drawing.
   b. a detail drawing.
   c. a block drawing.
   d. an installation drawing.

9. What type of drawing shows the wire size required for a particular installation?
   a. A block diagram   c. A wiring diagram
   b. A schematic diagram   d. A pictorial diagram

10. What type of diagram is used to explain a principle of operation, rather than show the parts as they actually appear?
    a. A pictorial diagram   c. A block diagram
    b. A schematic diagram   d. A wiring diagram

Chapter 7

1. Every body of matter in the universe attracts every other body with a certain force that is called

   _____.

2. The point at which all the weight of a body can be considered concentrated is called the

   _____.

3. The law that states, if a lever is in balance, the sum of the moments tending to turn the lever in one direction about an axis equals the sum of the moments tending to turn it in the opposite direction, is called the

   _____.

4. The tendency of a force to produce rotation around a given axis is called the _____ of the force with respect to that axis.

5. The _____ of an aircraft includes the weight of the airframe, power plant, required equipment that has a fixed location and is normally carried in the airplane, unusable fuel, and full operating fluids necessary for normal operation of aircraft systems such as oil and hydraulic fluid.

6. The maximum weight at which the aircraft may normally be landed is called the _____. weight.

7. Those points by which the airplane is supported at the time it is weighed are called the

   _____.

8. The product of the weight of an item multiplied by its arm is called the _____.

9. A location along the airplane fuselage given in terms of distance in inches from the reference datum is called

   a _____.

10. That portion of the oil in an aircraft lubricating system that will not drain from the engine with the aircraft in a level

    attitude is called _____.

11. The horizontal distance in inches from the datum to the center of gravity of the item is called the

    _____.

12. The algebraic sign of an arm is _____ if measured aft of the datum and _____ if measured forward of the datum.

13. Moments are expressed in _____.

14. The CG of the aircraft in its empty condition is called the _____.

15. The _____ is an imaginary vertical plane or line from which all horizontal measurements of arm are taken.

16. The abbreviation for the leading edge of the mean aerodynamic chord is called _____.

17. The maximum authorized weight of the aircraft and its contents as listed in the Type Certificate Data Sheet is called

    the _____.

18. The location of the datum is established by the _____.

19. The location of the datum may be found in the aircraft's _____.

20. The fuel that is available for flight planning purposes is called _____ fuel.

21. The empty weight used by air carriers as an average basic empty weight, which may be used for a group of aircraft of the same model and configuration, is called the _____ empty weight.

22. Those combinations of airplane weight and center of gravity that define the limits beyond which loading is not approved is referred to as the loading _____.

23. The maximum weight approved for ground maneuvers is called maximum _____ weight.

24. Fuel that cannot be consumed by the engine and is considered part of the aircraft's empty weight is called _____ fuel.

25. The distance between the forward and rearward limits within which the airplane must be operated is called the _____.

26. The reference points used by the aircraft technician to ensure that the aircraft is level for weight-and-balance purposes is called the _____.

27. For general weight-and-balance purposes the following weights are considered standard:

    a. Gasoline _____ lb/gal.

    b. Turbine fuel _____ lb/gal.

    c. Lubricating oil _____ lb/gal.

    d. Water _____ lb/gal.

    e. General aviation crew and passengers _____ lb

    f. Air carrier passenger (summer) _____ lb

    g. Air carrier passenger (winter) _____ lb

28. The weight of the equipment necessary for weighing the airplane (such as chocks, blocks, slings, jacks, etc.), which is included in the scale reading but is not a part of the actual weight of the airplane, is called _____ weight.

29. A vertical line passing through the center of the axle of the main landing gear wheel is the _____.

30. Tare weight must be _____ from the scale reading in order to obtain the actual weight of the airplane.

31. The abbreviation for the trailing edge of the mean aerodynamic chord is _____.

32. The minimum fuel for weight-and-balance computations is no more than the quantity of fuel required for _____ hour of operation at rated maximum continuous power. It is calculated on the maximum except takeoff (METO) horsepower.

33. _____ fuel is a part of the aircraft's empty weight.

34. The weight of the pilot, copilot, passengers, baggage, and usable fuel is called the aircraft's _____.

35. The maximum allowable weight at the start of the takeoff run is called maximum _____ weight.

36. The useful load is obtained by subtracting the _____ weight from the _____ weight.

37. The CG and CG limits may be expressed in terms of a percentage of the

_____ or in inches forward or to the rear of the

_____.

38. Normally, an aircraft will have acceptable flight characteristics if the CG is located somewhere near the _____ percent average chord point.

39. The aircraft should be weighed inside a closed building to avoid errors that may be caused by

_____.

40. An airplane must be in a _____ attitude to obtain accurate weighing information.

41. Leveling an aircraft is usually accomplished along both the _____ and

_____ axis.

42. When a new weight-and-balance report is prepared for an aircraft, the previous report should be marked

_____ and the date of the new document referenced.

43. The weight of any item installed in the airplane is _____.

44. The weight of any item removed from the airplane is _____.

45. When items are added forward of the datum line, the signs are (_____) weight × (_____) arm = (_____) moment.

46. When items are added to the rear of the datum line, the signs are (_____) weight × (_____) arm = (_____) moment.

47. When items are removed forward of the datum line, the signs are (_____) weight × (_____) arm = (_____) moment.

48. When items are removed to the rear of the datum line, the signs are (_____) weight × (_____) arm = (_____) moment.

49. The most important performance deficiencies of an overweight airplane are:

a. _____

b. _____

c. _____

d. _____

e. _____

f. _____

g. _____

h. _____

50. When too much weight is toward the forward part of the airplane, the center of gravity is shifted forward and any one of the following conditions may exist or they may occur in combination:

a. _____

b. _____

c. _____

d. _____

e. _____

f. _____

g. _____

51. When too much weight is toward the tail of the airplane, any one of the following conditions may exist or they may occur in combination:

a. _____

b. _____

c. _____

d. _____

e. _____

52. A weight-and-balance problem where the aircraft is loaded in a manner that will create the most critical balance condition while still remaining within the maximum gross weight of the aircraft is called an

_____ check.

53. In making a check of forward CG limit, it must be remembered that maximum weights for items forward of the

_____ CG limit are used as well as minimum weights for items to the rear of the

_____ CG limit.

54. To check an airplane for rearward CG limit, maximum weight for items located aft of the

_____ CG limit, and minimum weight for items forward of the _____
CG limit will be used.

55. An aircraft can have the empty-weight CG corrected by adding weight that is called _____ to the aircraft.

56. Most helicopters have a much more _____ CG range than do airplanes.

Chapter 7

Name _____

Date _____

APPLICATION QUESTIONS

1. Identify the location where the following weight and balance informational items are commonly found.

    A—Aircraft Weight-and-Balance Records
    B—Type Certificate Data Sheet
    C—Aircraft Maintenance Manual

    a. _____ Empty weight center of gravity

    b. _____ Location of the datum

    c. _____ Aircraft empty weight

    d. _____ Maximum gross weight

    e. _____ Unusable fuel

    f. _____ Center of gravity range

    g. _____ Leveling means

    h. _____ Detailed procedures for weighing the aircraft

    i. _____ Empty-weight CG range

    j. _____ Useful load

2. If a 40-lb generator applies +1400 in-lb to a reference axis, the generator is located

    _____ in from the axis.

3. Two boxes, which weigh 10 lb and 5 lb, are placed in an airplane so that their distances aft from the CG are 4 ft and 2 ft, respectively. How far forward of the CG should a third box, weighing 20 lb, be placed so that the CG will

    not be changed? _____ ft

4. An aircraft with an empty weight of 2100 lb and an empty-weight CG +32.5 was altered as follows:
    a. Two 18-lb passenger seats located at +73 were removed.
    b. Structural modifications were made at +77, increasing weight by 17 lb.
    c. A seat and safety belt weighing 25 lb were installed at +74.5.
    d. Radio equipment weighing 35 lb was installed at +95.

    What is the new empty-weight CG? _____ in

5. An aircraft as loaded weighs 4954 lb at a CG of +30.5 in. The CG range is +32.0 in to +42.1 in.
    Find the minimum weight of the ballast necessary to bring the CG within the CG range. The ballast arm is +162 in.

    _____ lb

6. As weighed, the total empty weight of an aircraft is 5862 lb with a moment of 885 957. However, when the aircraft was weighed, 20 lb of usable fuel was on board at +84.

    What is the empty-weight CG of the aircraft? _____ in

7. An aircraft with an empty weight of 1800 lb and an empty weight CG of +31.5 was altered as follows:
    a. Two 15-lb passenger seats located at +72 were removed.
    b. Structural modifications increasing the weight 14 lb were made at +76.
    c. A seat and safety belt weighing 20 lb were installed at +73.5.
    d. Radio equipment weighing 30 lb was installed at +30.

    What is the new empty-weight CG? _____ in

8. An aircraft had an empty weight of 2886 lb with a moment of 101 673.78 before several alterations were made. The alterations included:
   a. Removing two passenger seats (15 lb each) at +71.
   b. Installing a cabinet (97 lb) at +71.
   c. Installing a seat and safety belt (20 lb) at +71.
   d. Installing radio equipment (30 lb) at +94.

   The alterations caused the new empty-weight CG to move _____ in aft of the original empty-weight CG.

9. Datum is forward of the main gear center point: 83.25 in
   Actual distance between tail gear and main gear center points: 52.65 in
   Net weight at right main gear: 487 lb
   Net weight at left main gear: 467 lb
   Net weight at tail gear: 193 lb
   These items were in the aircraft when weighed:

   Fuel 28 gal., 2.8 gal. unusable at 35.1 in

   What is the empty-weight CG of the aircraft? _____ in.

10. When an empty aircraft is weighed, the combined net weight at the main gears is 3540 lb with an arm of 195.5 in. At the nose gear, the net weight is 2322 lb with an arm of 83.5 in. The datum line is forward of the nose of the aircraft.

    What is the empty-weight CG of the aircraft? _____ in.

11. An aircraft with an empty weight of 1500 lb and an empty-weight CG of +28.4 was altered as follows:
    a. Two 12-lb seats located at +68.5 were removed.
    b. Structural modifications weighing +28 lb were made at +73.
    c. A seat and safety belt weighing 30 lb were installed at +70.5.
    d. Radio equipment weighing 25 lb was installed at +85.

    What is the new empty-weight CG? _____ in

12. The following alteration was performed on an aircraft: A model B engine weighing 175 lb was replaced by a model D engine weighing 185 lb at a −62.00-in station. The aircraft weight-and-balance records show the previous empty weight to be 998 lb and an empty-weight CG of 13.48 in.

    What is the new empty-weight CG? _____ in.

13. The empty-weight CG location of the aircraft is 79.22 in.
    LEMAC is 60.0 in.
    TEMAC is 90.0 in.

    a. What is the length of the mean aerodynamic chord? _____ in

    b. What is the empty-weight CG expressed as a percent of MAC? _____ %

Chapter 7

Name _____

Date _____

Circle the letter of the best answer.

1. Which of the following tasks are completed prior to weighing an aircraft to determine its empty weight?
   a. Remove all items except those on the aircraft equipment list; drain usable fuel and fill hydraulic reservoir.
   b. Remove all items except those on the aircraft equipment list; drain usable fuel and hydraulic fluid.
   c. Remove all items on the aircraft equipment list; drain unusable fuel, compute oil and hydraulic fluid weight.
   d. Remove all items on the aircraft equipment list; drain fuel and hydraulic fluid.

2. The "maximum weight" as used in weight and balance control of a given aircraft can normally be found
   a. in the Aircraft Specifications or Type Certificate Data Sheets.
   b. by weighing the aircraft to obtain empty weight and mathematically adding the weight of fuel, oil, pilot, passengers, and baggage.
   c. by adding the empty weight and payload.
   d. in the back of the Aircraft Logbook.

3. The most important reason for aircraft weight and balance control in today's aircraft is
   a. to reduce noise levels.
   b. safety.
   c. to increase payloads.
   d. efficiency in flight.

4. How is the tare weight dealt with when weighing an aircraft?
   a. Subtracted from the zero fuel weight
   b. Added to the scale reading
   c. Subtracted from the scale reading
   d. Added to the maximum allowable gross weight

5. What information is *not* found in the aircraft Type Certificate Data Sheet?
   a. Empty weight
   b. Datum location
   c. Maximum weight
   d. Leveling means

6. Center of gravity equals
   a. Total weight/total moment
   b. Total moment/total weight
   c. Total moment/total arm
   d. Total weight/total arm

7. When computing weight and balance, an airplane is considered to be in balance when
   a. the movement of the passengers will not cause the moment arms to fall outside the CG range.
   b. the pilot is able to compensate for unbalance by use of elevator trim.
   c. the center of gravity of the loaded airplane falls within its CG range.
   d. all moment arms of the plane fall within CG range.

8. An airplane's EWCG could be found
   a. in the Type Certificate Data Sheet.
   b. in the Aircraft Specifications.
   c. in Note 2 of the TCDS.
   d. in the aircraft weight and balance records.

9. The reference datum line is often placed ahead of the aircraft because
   a. all arms will be positive numbers, contributing to accuracy.
   b. all manufacturers have agreed on this point for purposes of standardization.
   c. measurement of arms from the nose involves less movement of cargo.
   d. this is the only location from which all arms can be measured.

10. An aircraft is loaded with its present CG located aft of the aft CG limit. Which of the following is true?
    a. Removing weight aft of the present CG will help correct this condition.
    b. The CG cannot be corrected without adding fixed ballast.
    c. Shift weight from the front seats to the back seats to correct this condition.
    d. This condition cannot be corrected.

11. When dealing with weight and balance of an aircraft, the term maximum weight is interpreted to mean the maximum
    a. weight of the empty aircraft.
    b. weight of the useful load.
    c. authorized weight of the aircraft and its contents.
    d. weight of all optional or special equipment that can be installed in the aircraft.

12. Which of the following is considered TARE weight?
    a. Weight of required equipment installed in the airplane
    b. Oil in the engine
    c. Optional equipment installed in the airplane
    d. The weight of chocks used to hold the airplane on the scales

13. An aircraft useful load can be found in the
    a. aircraft weight-and-balance records.
    b. Type Certificate Data Sheet.
    c. last Form 337 filed.
    d. placard on the dash.

14. Installing a tail wheel on an aircraft that is 10 lb heavier than the one it replaced will
    a. cause the EWCG to shift forward.
    b. cause the EWCG to shift aft and empty weight to increase.
    c. cause the EW to decrease and move aft.
    d. cause the EWCG to remain unchanged.

15. The amount of fuel used for computing empty weight and corresponding center of gravity is
    a. empty fuel tanks.
    b. unusable fuel.
    c. full fuel tanks.
    d. the amount of fuel necessary for $\frac{1}{2}$ h of operation.

16. Weighing an aircraft outside is not recommended because
    a. the aircraft must be drained of fuel.
    b. the weighing equipment is not portable.
    c. it is too difficult to level the aircraft.
    d. air currents may affect the scale readings.

17. An aircraft that is loaded forward of its forward CG limit
    a. will have increased fuel consumption.
    b. will have increased stress on the nose gear.
    c. will have increased tendency to dive.
    d. All of the above

18. A CG of 178 in aft of the datum and a CG of 21 percent MAC
    a. represent LEMAC and TEMAC for the King Air.
    b. could represent the same state of balance.
    c. represent MAC for the average business jet.
    d. All of the above

19. The center of gravity of an aircraft is
    a. the point about which an aircraft will balance if suspended.
    b. horizontal to the longitudinal axis.
    c. perpendicular to the vertical axis.
    d. a reference point usually referred to as a datum line.

20. The useful load of a Part 23 certificated aircraft consists of the
    a. crew, passengers, fuel, oil, cargo, and fixed equipment.
    b. crew, power plant, fuel, oil, cargo, and passengers.
    c. crew, fuel, passengers, and cargo.
    d. crew, fuel, oil, and fixed equipment.

21. The empty weight of an airplane is determined by
    a. adding the gross weight on each weighing point and multiplying by the measured distance to the datum.
    b. adding the net weight of each weighing point and multiplying the measured distance to the datum.
    c. subtracting the tare weight from the scale reading and adding the weight of each weighing point.
    d. multiplying the measured distance from each weighing point to the datum times the sum of the scale reading less the tare weight.

22. What term is used to designate the distance an item is located from the datum in weight and balance computation?
    a. CG
    b. Moment
    c. MAC
    d. Arm

23. In the theory of weight and balance, the influence of weight is directly dependent upon its distance from the
    a. centerline of the aircraft.
    b. center of the fuselage.
    c. center of gravity.
    d. center of longitudinal axis.

24. Before weighing an aircraft, it is necessary to become familiar with the old aircraft empty weight and empty-weight CG in the weight and balance information located in
    a. the particular aircraft's weight and balance records.
    b. Advisory Circular 43.13-1A, Chap. 12.
    c. the applicable Aircraft Specification or Type Certificate Data Sheet.
    d. the manufacturer's service bulletins and letters.

25. When preparing an aircraft for weighing, which of the following should be filled unless otherwise noted in the aircraft specifications or manufacturer's instructions?
    a. Hydraulic reservoirs
    b. Fuel tanks
    c. Wash water reservoirs
    d. Drinking water reservoirs

26. (1) Private aircraft are required by regulations to be weighed periodically.
(2) Private aircraft are required to be weighed after making any alteration.

Regarding the above statements, which of the following is true?
a. Neither No. 1 nor No. 2 is true.
b. Only No. 1 is true.
c. Only No. 2 is true.
d. Both No. 1 and No. 2 are true.

27. How is the moment of an item about the datum obtained?
a. Arm times the item weight
b. Item weight times its distance from the loaded CG
c. Item weight times its distance from the empty CG
d. From the Aircraft Specifications or Type Certificate Data Sheets

28. When making a rearward weight and balance to determine that the CG will not exceed the rearward limit during extreme conditions, the items of useful load, which should be computed at their minimum weights, are located forward of the
a. forward CG limit.
b. empty-weight CG.
c. datum.
d. rearward CG limit.

29. When computing the maximum forward loaded CG of an aircraft, minimum weights, arms, and moments should be used for items of useful load that are located aft of the
a. rearward CG limit.
b. forward CG limit.
c. datum.
d. empty-weight CG.

30. To obtain useful weight data for purposes of determining the CG, it is necessary that an aircraft be weighed
a. with the main weighing points located within the normal CG limits.
b. in a level flight attitude.
c. with all items of useful load installed.
d. with at least minimum fuel (1/12-gal. per METO horsepower) in the fuel tanks.

31. What determines whether the value of the moment is preceded by a plus (+) or a minus (−) sign in aircraft weight and balance?
a. The addition or removal of weight
b. The location of the weight in reference to the datum
c. The result of a weight being added or removed and its location relative to the datum
d. The location of the datum in reference to the aircraft CG

32. Which of the following should be clearly indicated on the aircraft weighing form?
a. Minimum allowable gross weight.
b. Weight of unusable fuel.
c. Weighing points location.
d. Zero fuel weight.

33. The CG range in single-rotor helicopters is
a. in a location that prevents external loads from being carried.
b. much greater than for airplanes.
c. approximately the same as the CG range for airplanes.
d. more restricted than for airplanes.

34. If the empty-weight CG of an airplane lies within the empty-weight CG limits
a. it is necessary to calculate CG extremes.
b. it is not necessary to calculate CG extremes.
c. a loading schedule will not be required.
d. minimum fuel should be used in both forward and rearward CG checks.

Chapter 8

STUDY QUESTIONS

1. _____ is the ability of a material to be deformed without rupture or failure.

2. The _____ of a material refers to its plasticity under a tension or pulling load.

3. The rolling of metal into a thin sheet is possible due to its _____.

4. A _____ material is one that can not be visibly deformed and will shatter or break under load.

5. The _____ is the maximum amount of deformation that can occur with the material still returning to its original shape.

6. An operational definition of hardness is the resistance to _____.

7. Toughness is a desirable characteristic of the material to resist _____ or breaking when it is bent or stretched.

8. Stress may be defined as an internal force that resists the _____ of a material resulting from an external load.

9. The different types of stress are _____, _____, bending, _____, and shear.

10. Tension stress is the result of a _____ that tends to pull apart or stretch the material.

11. Compression stress occurs when the load _____ together or tends to _____ an object.

12. _____ stress results when two layers of a material are pulled apart.

13. Bending stress is a combination of _____ types of stress in a member.

14. Torsion stress is the result of a _____ force.

15. Stresses caused by a load acting perpendicular to the plane of the structural member are called _____ stresses.

16. Material placed under a compression load will usually fail by _____ or _____ rather than by compressive failure.

17. The point at which permanent deformation first occurs is known as the _____ point.

18. The modulus of elasticity is the value obtained by dividing the _____ by the _____.

19. A joint will fail in one of four ways: _____ failure of the material, shear failure of the fastener, _____ failure of the material, or _____ of the material.

20. Density combined with the strength characteristics of a material produces what is known as the _____ ratio of a material.

21. _____ conductivity is the property of a material to conduct heat. _____ conductivity is a measure of the material's ability to have electron flow.

22. _____ expansion refers to dimensional changes that occur as materials change temperature.

23. During the process of _____, atoms of a metal will arrange themselves in an orderly manner called a _____.

24. The widely used metals form either a _____ or _____-shaped space lattice.

25. Some metals crystallize in one atom arrangement upon further cooling change to another form. This is called an _____ change.

26. Within a metallic crystal are planes called _____ planes along which the atoms will move in relation to one another when an _____ load is applied.

27. A _____ grain metal is usually tougher and stronger than one with a _____ grain.

28. As a metal is cold-worked the material will become _____ and _____.

29. The effects of cold-working can be removed by a process known as _____ or _____.

30. A _____ solid solution alloy occurs when the _____ atom takes the place of a _____ atom in the lattice structure.

31. An _____ solid solution alloy occurs when the _____ atom wedges into the open space between the _____ atoms.

32. A _____ alloy occurs when you have _____ solubility in both the liquid and solid states.

33. When two elements form a Type I alloy, the product will be _____ and _____ than either element.

34. A _____ eutectic alloy is the result of combining two elements that have _____ solubility in the liquid state and _____ solubility in the solid state.

35. Type II alloys will have properties _____ between the two elements.

36. If two elements form a compound, the _____ properties of the elements are replaced by new ones characteristic of that compound; therefore the new properties _____ be predicted from the properties of the single elements.

37. Corrosion is the decomposition of metallic elements into compounds such as oxides, sulfates, hydroxides, and chlorides caused by _____ and _____ action.

38. Metal fatigue refers to the loss of _____ exhibited by a material as the number of _____, or load _____ increase.

39. Aluminum is the principal _____ metal for aircraft.

40. _____ aluminum is metal mechanically worked into the desired form by rolling, drawing, and extruding.

41. Wrought aluminum alloys are designated by a _____-digit system, with the first digit of the number indicating the principal _____.

42. The addition of _____ allows aluminum to be heat-treated to high strengths, but also _____ its corrosion resistance.

43. A letter and number combination is placed after the _____ code to indicate the processes that have taken place and the degree of _____.

44. The T designations are used after alloys capable of being hardened by _____ treatment.

45. Solution _____ is a thermal process for hardening aluminum.

46. Clad aluminum alloys have a thin layer of _____ rolled on each side to make the material more _____ resistant.

47. Aluminum alloy _____ in general has the highest strength of the non-heat-treatable alloys.

48. Aluminum alloy _____ is used to make rivets for riveting magnesium sheet.

49. A "modification" of alloy 2017, alloy _____ is used exclusively for the manufacture of aluminum rivets.

50. Aluminum alloy _____ is considered the standard structural metal for aircraft.

51. Aluminum alloy _____ is one of the highest-strength aluminum alloys available and one of the more difficult to work.

52. Ferrous metals are those whose principal content is _____.

53. A medium-carbon steel contains _____ to _____ percent carbon.

54. The higher the _____ content of steel, the greater its hardness and

_____.

55. The most common steel for aircraft structural purposes is SAE _____ chrome-moly steel.

56. The most important characteristics of stainless steels are _____ resistance, strength,

_____, and resistance to _____ temperatures.

57. Stainless steels can be divided into three general groups based on their chemical structure:

_____, _____, and _____.

58. Austenitic stainless steels can be _____ only by cold working, and heat treatment serves only

to _____ them.

59. Ferritic stainless steels contain no _____.

60. Martensitic stainless steels can be _____ by heat treatment.

61. The expansion of stainless steel due to temperature increases may be more than _____ that of ordinary carbon steels.

62. A major advantage of magnesium is that it is one of the _____ metals for its strength.

63. A major disadvantage of the use of magnesium is that it is more subject to _____ than many metals.

64. Titanium and its alloys are widely used in the aerospace industry because of their _____

strength, _____ weight, and high _____ resistance.

65. Titanium is equal to steel in _____ at approximately _____ of the weight.

66. When titanium is exposed to temperatures of 1000°F and above, it must be protected from the

_____, because at these temperatures it combines rapidly with _____.

67. At about _____, titanium will ignite in the presence of oxygen and

_____ with an incandescent flame.

68. The principal alloys with a copper base are _____, _____, and

_____ copper.

69. High-temperature alloys contain elements that make them particularly resistant to heat and corrosion and retain high tensile strength at elevated temperatures such as _____ to _____.

70. Plastics are classified as _____ resins or _____ resins.

71. Thermosetting resins _____ when heat of the correct value is applied.

72. Thermoplastic resins can be _____ by heat and _____.

73. Laminates are made by _____ a resin-saturated fabric over, or within, a _____ to produce a desired shape.

74. A laminate will be made up of a number of individual _____, called _____, of the fabric.

75. The resin, which _____ the plies together and provides stiffness, is usually referred to as the _____.

76. The most commonly used form of reinforcing material is _____.

77. A _____ fabric has most of the fibers running parallel to the warp and thus its _____ lies in the same direction.

78. Bidirectional fabric is woven to provide strength in _____ directions.

79. Kevlar is the registered trademark of _____ for an _____ fiber.

80. The matrix _____ the fibers together and transfers the _____ among the fibers.

81. Preimpregnated fabrics are those that have the _____ system impregnated into the fabric by _____.

82. Sandwich materials are constructed using high-strength material for _____, and a lightweight, lower-strength material for a _____.

83. Honeycomb _____ material has a core made of corrugated material assembled in a way that resembles a _____.

84. A solid core material uses a low-density material such as _____ wood or expanded _____ materials.

85. Three forms of wood are commonly used in aircraft: _____ wood, _____, and _____ wood.

86. The standard species of solid wood for aircraft use is _____.

87. The strength of wood will vary _____ with the density.

88. The dimensional change of a board due to moisture content will be the _____ across the fibers and _____ to the growth rings.

89. Checks are longitudinal cracks extending _____ annual rings. Shakes are _____ cracks _____ annual rings.

90. Unlike plywood, _____ wood has the grain running the _____ direction in all layers.

91. The FAA allows _____ wood spars to be replaced with _____ wood spars or vice versa if the material is of the same quality.

92. Aircraft-grade plywood is made of imported African _____ or American

_____ veneers laminated to cores of poplar or basswood with waterproof glue.

93. Grade A cloth is required on fabric-covered airplanes with wing loading in excess of _____ or

a never-exceed speed in excess of _____ mph.

94. Grade A cloth must have a tensile strength of _____ when new. It may be allowed to

deteriorate to _____ (70 percent) in use before being replaced.

Chapter 8

APPLICATION QUESTIONS

FORMULAS

Tensile Strength: $f = \frac{P}{A}$

Strain: $e = \frac{\Delta L}{L}$

Joint failure:

tensile	$P_{\text{tensile failure}}$	$= f_t \times [A - N(t \times D)]$
shear	$P_{\text{shear failure}}$	$= f_s \times A \times N$
bearing	$P_{\text{bearing failure}}$	$= f_b \times t \times D$
tearout	P_{tearout}	$= 2 \times (f_s \times t \times ed)$

---

1. A piece of material is 10 in wide and 0.063 in thick. What load would this material withstand before failing if it has an ultimate yield strength of 63 000 psi?

   Answer: _____

2. A fastener is $\frac{3}{16}$ in. in diameter and has a shear strength of 42 000 psi. What load will cause shear failure to occur?

   Answer: _____

3. A piece of material measures 6 in. in length, 0.040 in. in thickness, and 1 in. in width. After being loaded with 1000 lb it measured 6.050 in. (a) What amount of strain has occurred and (b) what is the amount of stress producing this strain?

   Answer: a. _____   b. _____

4. Which material would have the better strength-to-weight ratio: material A with a density of 0.28 lb per cubic inch and a tensile strength of 83 000 psi or material B with a density of 0.172 lb per cubic inch with a tensile strength of 37 000 psi?

   Answer: _____

5. A simple lap joint has two pieces 0.050 in by 2 in with two fasteners $\frac{1}{8}$ in. in diameter. The material tensile strength is 32 500 psi, bearing strength is 85 000, and shear strength is 28 000 psi. The fasteners have a shear strength of 37 000 psi. The fasteners are $\frac{3}{8}$ in from the edge of the sheet. (a) At what load and (b) how would this joint fail?

   Answer: a. _____   b. _____

Match the series number and the alloy element.

6. _____ 1000   A. Copper

7. _____ 2000   B. Magnesium

8. _____ 3000   C. Magnesium/silicon

9. _____ 5000   D. Manganese

10. _____ 6000   E. Zinc

11. _____ 7000   F. Pure aluminum

Write the suffix letter that would describe the following:

12. As fabricated (no treatment) _____

13. Annealed _____

14. Cold worked or strain hardened _____

15. Unstable condition _____

16. Solution heat-treated only _____

17. Solution heat-treated, cold worked _____

18. Solution heat-treated and artificially aged _____

Chapter 8

Name _____

Date _____

Circle the letter of the best answer.

1. Which of the following is not a characteristic of a metal?
   a. A crystalline structure
   b. High reflectivity
   c. A high (+2000°F) melting point.
   d. An ability to be deformed.

2. Which type of unit cell would exhibit the least amount of ductility?
   a. BCC   b. FCC   c. CPH   d. HEX

3. An allotropic metal is one that
   a. may have more than one crystalline structure.
   b. will melt at the lowest temperature.
   c. will dissolve a second material in a solid state.
   d. can withstand a high range of temperatures.

4. The core material of Alclad 2024-T4 is
   a. commercially pure aluminum, and the surface material is strain-hardened aluminum alloy.
   b. heat-treated aluminum alloy, and the surface material is commercially pure aluminum.
   c. commercially pure aluminum, and the surface material is heat-treated aluminum alloy.
   d. strain-hardened aluminum alloy, and the surface material is commercially pure aluminum.

5. The aluminum code number 1100 identifies what type of aluminum?
   a. Aluminum alloy containing 11 percent copper.
   b. Heat-treated aluminum alloy.
   c. Aluminum alloy containing zinc.
   d. 99 percent commercially pure aluminum.

6. In the four-digit aluminum index system number 2024, the first digit indicates
   a. zinc has been added to the aluminum.
   b. the different alloys in that group.
   c. the percent of alloys added.
   d. copper is the major alloying element.

7. The Society of Automotive Engineers and the American Iron and Steel Institute use a numerical index system to identify the composition of various steels. The symbol 1020 indicates a plain carbon steel containing an average of
   a. 20.00 percent carbon.
   b. 2.00 percent carbon by volume.
   c. 2.00 percent carbon by weight.
   d. 0.20 percent carbon by weight.

8. The corrosion protection of stainless steel is provided primarily by
   a. chromium   c. molybdenum
   b. nickel   d. titanium

9. Bronze is an alloy of copper and
   a. beryllium   c. tin
   b. zinc   d. aluminum

10. The lightest structural metal used in aircraft is
    a. magnesium b. aluminum c. titanium d. brass

11. Which of the following is not true of titanium?
    a. It provides excellent corrosion resistance.
    b. It weighs more than aluminum but less than steel.
    c. It is easily worked.
    d. It is excellent for temperatures to 800°F.

12. Unidirectional fiberglass cloth has
    a. an equal number of threads in warp and fill.
    b. a greater number of threads in warp.
    c. a greater number of threads in all directions.
    d. equal strength in all directions.

13. Ceramic cloth is rated as the poorest of the composite fabrics in terms of
    a. toughness.   c. weight.
    b. heat resistance. d. strength.

14. Laminated wood is often used in the construction of highly stressed aircraft components. This wood can be identified by its
    a. increased resistance to deflection.
    b. parallel grain construction.
    c. similarity to standard plywood construction.
    d. alternate perpendicular ply construction.

15. Grade A fabric must be used if the aircraft
    a. has a never-exceed speed greater than 160 mph.
    b. has a wing loading of less than 9 lb per square foot.
    c. Both A and B are correct answers.
    d. Neither A nor B is correct.

Chapter 9

STUDY QUESTIONS

1. Aluminum alloy sheet, as it comes from the manufacturer, is marked with _____ and _____ in rows about 6 in apart.

2. Hot working involves _____ deformation of the metal at a temperature that results in the metal being continually _____.

3. Cast products are formed by _____ the metal and pouring it into a _____ of the desired shape.

4. Rolling is a widely used process of plastic deformation that _____ the thickness of metal by subjecting it to _____ forces by passing it between driven cylindrical _____.

5. Many hot-rolled materials may be identified by the presence of a hard, _____ scale formed by the _____ in the atmosphere combining with the _____ of the hot metal.

6. Cold-rolled metals will usually have a _____, natural _____ finish.

7. Forging is a process in which the metal is forced to _____ under high _____ stresses.

8. The _____ process uses compressive force to cause the metal to flow through a die.

9. Bending is a forming process in which plastic deformation occurs only in a relatively _____ area along a bend line.

10. Die drawing is commonly used for _____ and tubes.

11. Continuous roll forming is a process of forming shapes such as angles and channels by passing a _____ of sheet metal through a _____ of rollers.

12. Spinning involves the forming of a _____ part over a mandrel with a tool or roller.

13. Shearing is a process for separating (cutting) a metal by forcing two _____ and slightly _____ blades against it, with sufficient force to cause _____.

14. Annealing is accomplished by heating the metal to a temperature that allows new _____ formation to occur.

15. All metals are affected by _____ working, and all metals will respond to _____ treatments.

16. Some metals are allotropic; that is, their _____ structure will change at elevated temperatures.

17. Hardening of aluminum is accomplished by alloying an element that is _____ only at higher temperatures.

18. To be hardened by heat treatment, aluminum must have _____ as an alloy.

19. At lower temperatures the copper alloy _____ as a metallic compound, producing _____ effects.

20. The first step of heat treatment for aluminum is to heat the aluminum to allow the alloy to enter into a _____ solution.

21. The second step of heat treatment for aluminum is to cool, or _____, the material as _____ as possible.

22. The precipitation process can be _____ by reheating the material and allowing it to soak for a specified time. This is known as artificial _____.

23. The formation of larger compound particles, because of _____ cooling, presents the potential of dissimilar metals causing _____ corrosion.

24. Although 2024 alloy ages very quickly, the precipitation process may be _____ by _____ storage.

25. Aluminum is annealed by _____ to the required temperature, allowing it to _____ for the time necessary for recrystallization to occur, and cooling the metal _____.

26. Ferrous metals can be hardened by heat treatment only if _____ is an alloy.

27. Unlike aluminum, steel can be _____ and _____ to a range of values.

28. When carbon steel is heated to a temperature of 1341°F, a solid solution of iron and _____, consisting of 0.76 percent carbon, called _____ is formed.

29. If a carbon steel contains less than 0.76 percent carbon, the result will be a mixture of _____ and _____.

30. Ferrite is almost pure iron of relatively _____ tensile strength with a maximum of 0.025 percent _____.

31. When austenite is cooled below 1341°F, a compound of iron carbide (Fe$_3$), called _____, precipitates from the solution at the crystal _____.

32. As cooling continues, the austenite decomposes into alternate platelets of _____ and _____ in a form called _____.

33. Rapid cooling of austenite precludes the formation of _____, and the austenite changes immediately to a structure called _____.

34. The hardening process is performed by heating the metal slightly above its _____ temperature and then _____ cooling it.

35. It is usually necessary to _____ the steel to achieve the necessary toughness and to _____ brittleness.

36. Tempering consists of _____ the hardened steel to a temperature _____ the critical range, holding this temperature for a sufficient period, then cooling.

37. The degree of _____ obtained by tempering depends directly upon the temperatures to which the steel is heated.

38. When _____ temperatures are used for tempering, ductility is _____ at the expense of hardness and tensile strength.

39. The normalizing process _____ stresses in the metal that have been caused by production process.

40. Steel products can be fully annealed by _____ to the appropriate temperatures and cooling _____.

41. Case _____ processes produce a hard, wear-resisting surface, while leaving the core of the metal _____ and resilient.

42. Three common methods of case hardening are _____, _____, and _____.

43. Magnesium alloy castings are _____ heat _____ to improve such characteristics as tensile strength, ductility, and shock resistance.

44. The temperatures to which magnesium alloys are heated for heat treatment are _____ than those used for aluminum alloys.

45. Heat treatment for titanium is possible for _____ alloys and _____ for others.

46. Hardness is used as an indication of _____ for many materials.

47. The Brinell hardness test is performed by forcing a steel _____ into the material. The reading is taken by measuring the _____ of the _____ made in the material.

48. The Rockwell hardness test is made by using either a _____ point, or a ball of fixed size, under a predetermined load.

49. The Vickers test uses a _____ pyramid for a penetrator and is particularly useful for testing very _____ steels.

50. Nondestructive inspection (NDI) refers to a number of methods that have been developed to _____ and measure the extent of a _____ without damaging the component.

51. A gas _____ in the molten metal during manufacturing may lead to a _____ discontinuity in the finished part.

52. Cracks in a component may be the result of _____ and _____ buildup during machining.

53. Common to all methods of NDI is that the part to be tested must be _____ and _____ of foreign objects.

54. Magnetic particle inspection is a method of detecting cracks or other flaws on the _____ or _____ of materials that are readily magnetized.

55. A defect at a right angle to the magnetic lines will show up _____. Defects parallel to the magnetic lines will show _____.

56. Longitudinal magnetization is normally accomplished by placing the part in a _____.

57. Circular magnetization is accomplished by passing the electric current directly _____ the part.

58. Disruptions of the magnetic lines of force are not visible. To make them visible, small _____ particles are used.

59. The penetrant process involves the use of a penetrating _____ that _____ into cracks or other defects.

60. Penetrant inspection can be used on any material but will detect only _____ defects, or _____ defects if they are open to the _____.

61. Fluorescent-penetrant inspection uses a fluorescent penetrant that when viewed under a _____ light (ultraviolet) will make the indications _____ to see.

62. When an electrically conductive material is subjected to an alternating _____ field, small circulating electric currents, called _____ currents, are generated in the material.

63. The eddy currents generate their own magnetic _____, which interacts with the magnetic field of the coil, or probe, influencing the _____, or opposition to current flow in the coil.

64. By monitoring the impedance of the coil, tests can be made to _____ flaws in metal, _____ metals on the basis of alloy, temper, or other metallurgical conditions, and _____ according to size, shape, thickness.

65. Ultrasonic inspection utilizes high-frequency _____ to reveal flaws in metal parts.

66. Radiography uses powerful X-ray machine to produce _____ that penetrate metal and impinge upon a _____ plate. Flaws in the metal will be revealed as _____ in the picture of the part.

67. Chemical _____ is brought about by an acid, salt, or alkali in the presence of _____.

68. Electrolytic corrosion takes place when metals that have different levels of _____ are touching or in close proximity in the presence of moisture.

69. Surface corrosion on aluminum generally appears as _____ blotches if on the surface and as small, _____ lumps if it has penetrated below the clad surface and is attacking the interior of the metal.

70. The higher the metal is on the electrochemical series list, the _____ active it is and the _____ susceptible to corrosive activity. When dissimilar metals are in contact, the _____ active metal will be destroyed.

71. Intergranular corrosion is caused by improper _____.

72. Stress corrosion results when a metal part is _____ stressed over a long period of time under _____ conditions.

73. Fretting corrosion occurs when there is _____ movement between close-fitting metal parts.

74. The repair of parts affected by corrosion but not rendered unserviceable is a matter of removing the existing _____ products and applying a coating or finish that will _____ further corrosion.

75. Parts made of carbon or alloy steel that are not highly stressed can be cleaned with buffers, _____ brushes, sandblasting, steel _____, or _____ papers.

76. When removing corrosion from aluminum parts, the use of _____ wire brushes, _____ wool, _____ cloth, or other harsh abrasives should be avoided.

77. Mild abrasives or polish can be used on clad aluminum alloy but must not be used for cleaning _____ alloys.

78. Structural aluminum-alloy parts that have suffered severe intergranular corrosion must usually be

_____.

79. Since magnesium is the most chemically _____ of the metals employed in aircraft, it is also

the most _____ with respect to corrosion.

80. Many manufacturers in the aerospace industry have adopted the _____
(rms) microinch system to designate surface roughness.

81. Corrosion treatments for aluminum alloys provide the material with a protective _____.

82. Magnesium is usually treated with a chrome pickle or _____
process for corrosion protection.

83. Steel parts are protected by _____ plating or _____ plating processes,

which protect the surface from _____.

84. Cadmium plating is a nonporous, _____ deposited layer of cadmium that offers high

_____ resistance for steel.

85. Anodizing, applied to aluminum by an acid plating process, _____ the surface, reduces

porosity, _____ abrasion resistance, and has high _____ strength.

Chapter 9

Name _____

Date _____

APPLICATION QUESTIONS

A. Bar   D. Plate   G. Sheet
B. Foil   E. Rod   H. Tube
C. Forging   F. Shape   J. Wire

Part 1: Match the mill product listed above with the descriptive terms below. A product term may be used more than once.

1. _____ A $\frac{3}{4}$-in square cross section with rounded corners and 0.063-in wall thickness.

2. _____ Rectangular in cross section with a thickness of 0.0035-in.

3. _____ Rectangular in cross section and with a thickness of 0.3125-in by 24-in wide.

4. _____ Rectangular in cross section and measuring 0.040-in by 48-in.

5. _____ An angle in cross section measuring $1\frac{1}{2}$-in by $1\frac{1}{2}$-in by $\frac{1}{4}$-in thick.

6. _____ A solid product rectangular in cross section measuring $\frac{1}{4}$-in by 1-in.

7. _____ A round hollow product with a 1-in outside diameter.

8. _____ A solid $\frac{1}{2}$-in. in diameter.

9. _____ A solid round cross section $\frac{5}{16}$-in in diameter.

10. _____ A solid regular hexagon in cross section measuring $\frac{3}{4}$-in across the flats.

Part 2: Use Tables 9–1 through 9–8 in the text to answer Questions 11 through 22.

11. What temperature range would be used to solution-heat-treat 6061 aluminum?

Answer: _____

12. What temperature range would be used to age the material in Question 11?

Answer: _____

13. What temper designation would be applied to the metal after performing the processes in Questions 11 and 12?

Answer: _____

14. What would be the soaking time for a piece of 7075 material that is $\frac{3}{32}$-in thick?

Answer: _____

15. What temperature should you use to remove the effects of cold working from 2024 aluminum alloy sheet?

Answer: _____

16. What temperature range would be used to anneal 4130 steel?

Answer: _____

17. What temperature range would be used to harden 2330 steel?

Answer: _____

18. What temperature would be used to temper 4130 steel to a 125 000-psi tensile strength?

Answer: _____

19. After tempering, the material in Question 18 is to be tested with a Rockwell tester using the A scale. What should the reading be?

Answer: _____

20. Performing the same test as in Question 19 with a Vickers tester would give what reading?

Answer: _____

21. If copper and steel are subjected to galvanic corrosion, which metal will be destroyed?

Answer: _____

22. Which material is more active in terms of corrosion, 2024 alloy or 7075 alloy?

Answer: _____

Chapter 9

REVIEW EXAM

Name _____

Date _____

Circle the letter of the best answer.

1. In order for dye penetrant inspection to be effective, the material being checked must
   a. have subsurface cracks.
   c. be magnetic.
   b. be nonmagnetic.
   d. have surface cracks.

2. Surface cracks in aluminum castings and forgings may usually be detected by
   a. the use of dye pentrants and suitable developers.
   b. heating the part to approximately 750° and observing the surface for any material that may have been forced out of a crack.
   c. magnetic particle inspection.
   d. submerging the part in a solution of hydrochloric acid and rinsing with clear water.

3. Which of these metals is inspected using the magnetic particle inspection method?
   a. Magnesium alloys
   c. Aluminum alloys
   b. Iron alloys
   d. Copper

4. Which type crack can be detected by magnetic particle inspection using either circular or longitudinal magnetization?
   a. 45°
   c. Longitudinal
   b. Transverse
   d. Circumferential

5. When checking an item with the magnetic particle inspection method, circular and longitudinal magnetization should be used to
   a. reveal all possible defects.
   b. prevent one-way polarization.
   c. prevent permanent magnetization.
   d. ensure uniform current flow.

6. If a pure metal is heated above its critical temperature and cooled to room temperature, it will
   a. form a mechanical mixture.
   b. return to its original structure.
   c. form a combination of a solid solution and mechanical mixture.
   d. form a complex solution.

7. What type of corrosion attacks grain boundaries of aluminum alloys that are improperly or inadequately heat-treated?
   a. Stress   b. Intergranular   c. Surface   d. Fretting

8. If too much time is allowed to elapse during the transfer of 2017 or 2024 aluminum alloy from the heat treatment medium to the quench tank, it may result in
   a. case hardening.
   b. a dull, stained, or streaked surface.
   c. retarded age hardening.
   d. impaired corrosion resistance.

9. Which heat-treating process of metal produces a hard, wear-resistant surface over a strong, tough core?
   a. Case hardening
   c. Annealing
   b. Tempering
   d. Normalizing

10. Nitriding is a process that
    a. forms a hard case on a part to resist wear.
    b. decreases the size of the grain structure.
    c. toughens steel to increase its tensile strength.
    d. increases bearing heat resistance.

11. What does *not* take place during the aging process of an aluminum alloy after solution heat treatment?
    a. The material becomes stronger.
    b. The material becomes harder.
    c. The material becomes more difficult to bend and form.
    d. The material becomes more resistant to corrosion.

12. Why is steel tempered after being hardened?
    a. To increase its hardness and ductility
    b. To decrease its ductility and brittleness
    c. To increase its strength and decrease its internal stresses
    d. To relieve its internal stresses and reduce its brittleness

13. What aluminum alloy designations indicate that the metal has been solution heat-treated and artificially aged?
    a. 3003-F   b. 7075-T6   c. 5052-H36   d. 6061-O

14. Which material cannot be heat-treated repeatedly without harmful effects?
    a. Unclad aluminum alloy in sheet form
    b. Products molded of steel
    c. 6061-T9 stainless steel
    d. Clad aluminum alloy

15. What will determine the hardness of steel at ordinary temperatures?
    a. The number of particles of iron carbide in the mixture
    b. The size of the particles of iron austenite in the mixture
    c. The distribution of the particles of iron matrix throughout the mixture
    d. The transformation of pearlite to austenite in the mixture

Chapter 10

STUDY QUESTIONS

1. The most widely used standards for aircraft hardware are _____ and _____.

2. Hardware items which have been proven satisfactory by the aerospace industry may be given a _____ (NAS) designation.

3. Aeronautical Standards (AS) have been established by the _____ of _____ (SAE).

4. A specification may be defined as a statement of particulars describing the _____, _____, or peculiarities of any work about to be undertaken.

5. A specification sets forth the standards of _____ and _____ that a particular aircraft or component must meet to be acceptable for the purpose intended.

6. The FAA requires all _____, aircraft _____, and _____ to be certificated.

7. The winding groove around a bolt, screw, or in the hole of a nut forms what is called a _____.

8. Aircraft hardware uses a design based upon a _____ thread.

9. The _____ diameter of an external thread is the diameter measured across the thread crest.

10. The minor diameter is the diameter at the _____ of the thread.

11. Pitch diameter is a standard value for a given thread size and is approximately _____ between the _____ and _____ diameter.

12. The _____ of a screw refers to the distance that the screw will advance into another threaded object with _____.

13. Threads are made in two series, unified national _____ (UNF) and unified national _____ (UNC).

14. Threaded fasteners larger than _____ diameter are dimensioned by fractions of an inch and those smaller are dimensioned by _____ sizes.

15. Machine screw sizes range from 0, the _____, to 12, the _____.

16. The screw threads for a bolt that is $\frac{3}{16}$-in. in diameter will use the threads specified for a _____ screw.

17. The fit between internal and external threads has been standardized into five classes ranging from No. 1, _____, to No. 5, _____.

18. Aircraft _____ utilize a class 3 thread, while aircraft _____ may use either a class 2 or 3 thread.

19. Bolts are designed to be used with a _____ and have a portion of the shank that is not threaded, called the _____.

20. Bolt sizes are expressed in terms of _____ and _____.

21. An all-purpose structural bolt used for both _____ and _____ loading is made under AN standards 3 through 20.

22. The _____ of the all-purpose bolt is specified by the AN number in _____ of an inch.

23. Bolts in the AN3 to 20 series are designed for use with a _____ nut and have a hole drilled in the shank for a _____.

24. All-purpose bolts are made of _____ steel, aluminum alloy and _____ steel.

25. The bolt's material can be identified by head markings; alloy steel bolts will have a cross, or _____, aluminum-alloy bolts will have _____ raised dashes, and a corrosion-resistant steel will have _____ raised dash.

26. The use of alloy steel bolts smaller than _____ in diameter and aluminum alloy bolts smaller than _____ in diameter are prohibited for use in aircraft _____ structure by the FAA.

27. FAA Advisory Circular 43.13-1A allows a general-purpose bolt to be used in place of the close-tolerance bolt if the bolt has a _____ fit in the hole.

28. Drilled-head engine bolts are designed to be installed into threads tapped in an _____.

29. Clevis bolts are designed only for _____ load applications.

30. Nuts are used to hold the _____ in place and provide the _____ force to make a strong joint.

31. One method of locking a nut to a bolt involves mechanically locking the two together with _____ wire or a _____ pin.

32. A second method of locking a nut and bolt together is to create _____ between the two threads.

33. The AN310 nut is shaped for a _____ to be used to mechanically lock the nut and bolt together.

34. The AN315 _____ nut has no special features but is available with either _____-hand or _____-hand threads.

35. Self-locking nuts are made with a nonmetallic _____ or with the top two or three threads _____.

36. The self-locking nut used with an AN3 bolt will have a dash number of _____.

37. Federal Aviation Regulations _____ the use of self-locking nuts on any bolt subject to _____ in operation unless a nonfriction locking device is used in _____ to the friction lock.

38. Washers serve three functions: to protect the material from being _____; to allow small adjustments of _____ length; and to provide a _____ force between the nut and the bolt.

39. The AN970 large-area flat washer was designed to be used with bolts in _____ structures and spread the clamping force over a larger area to keep the _____ fibers from being crushed.

40. The AN935 split-ring lock-washer is made of a _____ piece of steel to provide a _____ force to keep the nut tight.

41. The AN936 is a thin washer with a number of _____ teeth that are

_____ as the nut is tightened.

42. Cotter pins are used to lock _____ nuts onto _____ bolts or to secure plain-shank pins in a hole.

43. AN380 is the standard for _____ plated steel cotter pins with AN381 being the standard for

those made of _____ steel.

44. A screw has the shank _____ all the way to the head.

45. Most machine screws specified for aircraft have _____ threads with a class _____ fit.

An exception is the No. 10 screw, which has a fine thread compatible with nuts used for _____ bolts.

46. A head made for use with a Phillips screwdriver is called a _____ head and is available on all AN screws.

47. The AN507 flat head screw requires that the material in which it is placed have a _____ area.

48. The AN526 _____ head screw has a large head that provides a good

_____ force on thin sheet-metal parts.

49. The pan head screw has a large head _____ similar to the truss head, but with a thicker head

allowing for more _____ load.

50. The fillister head screw has a _____ head of a small _____ when compared to other screws.

51. Structural screws are made from alloy _____ and have a _____ length.

52. Self-tapping screws are also called _____ screws and are only used for applications.

53. Self-tapping screws are made in two styles: Type A with _____ points and Type B with

_____ points.

54. Flat head pins are used to join rod _____ to bellcranks, secondary-control-cable terminals to

control _____ or levers, or other situations where the control is not in continuous operation.

55. Rivets are designed primarily for _____ loads and are fastened in place by forming, or

_____, a second head on the shank.

56. As the rivet's upset head is formed, the shank will swell in _____ and completely fill the

hole, forming a very _____ joint.

57. The material from which a rivet has been made can be determined by the _____.

58. Alloy 2024 type DD must be _____ and quenched _____ prior to driving.

59. Alloy _____ type AD rivets may be driven ''off the shelf'' at any time.

60. Alloy 5056 type B rivets are used for riveting _____ sheet.

61. Rivets are sized by the _____ of their shanks and their _____.

62. Blind _____ are designed to be installed where access to both sides of a sheet assembly or structure is not possible.

63. Hole size is _____ for blind rivet installation because the rivet will not swell to

_____ the hole while being driven.

64. The Cherrylock rivet uses a _____ to lock the _____ into the rivet shell.

65. The _____ Cherrylock rivet forms a larger, bulbed head to provide more _____ force for thinner sheet metals.

66. The Cherrymax rivet is similar to the Cherrylock except it has been designed for easier _____.

67. A rivnut is a hollow blind _____ that serves as a nut and is used in many places where _____ are required but the metal is too _____ to be threaded.

68. A blind bolt can be completely installed from one side of a structure and is used when a high _____ strength is needed.

69. The Hi-Shear rivet has a _____ made of steel or other high-strength material and is held in place by a _____ collar of aluminum or other soft material.

70. Because there is no change in the _____ diameter during Hi-Shear installation, the _____ is very critical and may require reaming to size.

71. Lock-bolts are similar to the Hi-Shear rivet in function and are made in two types, the _____ type and the _____ type.

72. A Hi-Lok bolt is a _____ fastener with the features of the swaged collar-type fastener.

73. Panel and cowling fasteners such as the _____, _____, and _____ are important in the inspection and servicing of an aircraft.

74. It is a good practice to paint the _____ of the terminal or fitting and the cable to provide a means of detection for _____ cable at later inspections.

75. Turnbuckles are used for adjusting the _____ of control cables.

76. A standard turnbuckle consists of a _____ and two steel ends, one end having _____ -hand thread and the other having a _____ -hand thread.

77. The end of the turnbuckle barrel with left-hand threads is marked with a _____ completely around the end of the barrel.

78. When the turnbuckle is tightened, no more than _____ threads must show outside the barrel at each end.

79. All seats in an airplane that may be _____ during takeoff or landing must be equipped with _____ safety (seat) belts.

80. Each half of an approved safety-belt assembly must have legibly and permanently marked on or attached to it a _____ or _____ label.

Chapter 10

Name _____

Date _____

APPLICATION QUESTIONS

1. Write the designation for an AN general-purpose bolt $\frac{5}{16}$-in. in diameter with a length of $1\frac{1}{4}$ in. The shank is not drilled.

   Answer: _____

2. Write the designation for a fiber insert nut to be used with the bolt in Question 1.

   Answer: _____

3. Write the designation for a corrosion resistant $\frac{1}{4}$-in. by 1-in. bolt for use with a castellated nut.

   Answer: _____

4. Write the designation for a (1) nut and (2) flat washer to use with the bolt in Question 3.

   Answer: (1) _____   (2) _____

5. Write the designation for a $\frac{5}{16}$-in diameter close-tolerance bolt.

   Answer: _____

6. What is the AN designation for a stainless steel cotter pin to use with an AN7 bolt?

   Answer: _____

7. What is the designation for the correct size of carbon steel cotter pin for an AN3 bolt?

   Answer: _____

8. Write the designation for a clevis bolt that is $\frac{5}{16}$-in. in diameter by $\frac{3}{4}$-in. long?

   Answer: _____

9. What is the AN number for a fine thread fillister head screw with a class 2 fit?

   Answer: _____

10. Write the MS designation for a $\frac{5}{32}$-in. diameter by $\frac{7}{8}$-in-long rivet with a universal head made of 2024 alloy.

    Answer: _____

Chapter 10

Name _____

Date _____

Circle the letter of the best answer.

1. A fiber-type, self-locking nut should never be used on an aircraft if the bolt is
   a. under shear loading.
   b. subject to rotation.
   c. under tension loading.
   d. to be mounted in a vertical position.

2. Aircraft bolts with a cross or asterisk marked on the bolt head are
   a. made of stainless steel.
   b. close-tolerance bolts.
   c. made of aluminum alloy.
   d. standard steel bolts.

3. Which statement regarding aircraft bolts is correct?
   a. AN standard steel bolts are marked with two raised dashes.
   b. When tightening castellated nuts on drilled bolts, if the cotter pin holes do not line up, it is permissible to overtighten the nut to permit alignment of the next slot with the cotter pin hole.
   c. In general, bolt grip length should equal the material thickness.
   d. Alloy steel bolts smaller than $\frac{1}{4}$-in. diameter should not be used in the primary structure.

4. A bolt with a single raised dash on the head is classified as an
   a. AN corrosion-resistant steel bolt.
   b. NAS close-tolerance bolt.
   c. NAS standard aircraft bolt.
   d. AN aluminum alloy bolt.

5. Where is an AN clevis bolt used in an airplane?
   a. In landing-gear assemblies
   b. For tension and shear load conditions
   c. Where external tension loads are applied
   d. Only for shear load applications

6. A bolt with an X inside a triangle on the head is classified as an
   a. AN aluminum alloy bolt.
   b. NAS close-tolerance bolt.
   c. NAS standard aircraft bolt.
   d. AN corrosion-resistant steel bolt.

7. Aircraft bolts are usually manufactured with a
   a. class 1 fit for the threads.
   b. class 3 fit for the threads.
   c. class 2 fit for the threads.
   d. class 4 for fit the threads.

8. How is the locking feature of the fiber-type lock nut obtained?
   a. By a saw-cut fiber insert with a pinched-in thread in the locking section
   b. By the use of an nonthreaded fiber locking insert
   c. By a fiber insert held firmly in place at the base of the load-carrying section
   d. By placing the threads in the fiber insert out-of-phase with the load-carrying section

9. If a Hi-Shear rivet is underdriven during installation, the
   a. stud will not expand and fill the drilled hole properly.
   b. collar will be incompletely swaged into the groove.
   c. shear strength of the rivet will be reduced.
   d. stem will loosen, resulting in a hollow rivet shank.

10. Alloy 2117 rivets are heat-treated
    a. by the manufacturer and do not require heat treatment before being driven.
    b. by the manufacturer but require reheat treatment before being driven.
    c. to a temperature of 910 to 930° and quenched in cold water.
    d. to a temperature of 930 to 950° and quenched in cold water.

11. Pin (Hi-Shear) rivets have the same shear strength as
    a. solid shank AN470DD (icebox) rivets of the same diameter.
    b. bolts of equal diameter.
    c. hollow-core rivets of the same diameter.
    d. self-plugging friction lock rivets of equal diameter.

12. Self-plugging Cherry rivet shank diameters are measured in increments of
    a. $\frac{1}{16}$ in.   c. $\frac{1}{8}$ in.
    b. $\frac{3}{32}$ in.   d. $\frac{1}{32}$ in.

13. Bulbed Cherrylock rivet grip length is measured in increments of
   a. $\frac{1}{32}$ in.
   c. $\frac{3}{32}$ in.
   b. $\frac{1}{16}$ in.
   d. $\frac{1}{8}$ in.

14. The control cable terminals on most late-model aircraft are swaged and a painted band is placed around the cable adjacent to the terminal in order to
   a. ascertain if the cable is safetied properly.
   b. protect the cable and the fitting from electrolytic corrosion.
   c. disclose twisting of the cable in the fitting.
   d. detect slippage of the cable in the fitting.

15. If a new safety belt is to be installed in an aircraft, the belt must conform to the strength requirements in which of the following documents?
   a. STC 1282
   b. FAR Part 65
   c. FAR Part 39
   d. TSO C22

Chapter 11

STUDY QUESTIONS

1. Layout refers to the process of _____ measurements from a _____ to materials from which parts will be fabricated.

2. The _____ of the rule refers to how the units of length are marked off. The markings are referred to as _____.

3. The first step in reading a rule is to know the _____ of the _____ on the rule.

4. A caliper can be used as a _____ when machining a part to size by first setting it, with the aid of a _____, to the desired _____.

5. The legs of the divider are _____ and have sharp points. Dividers are designed to _____ a desired dimension from a _____ to a piece of material.

6. A _____ caliper has a scale located on a beam with one _____ jaw.

7. The jaws on a slide caliper are formed so that either _____ or _____ measurements can be made.

8. The basic micrometer unit is made up of three parts, a _____ or barrel, a _____, and a _____.

9. Micrometers are designed for a _____ of measurement of _____ inch.

10. The ability of the micrometer to measure to _____ inch is based on the fact that it has a spindle threaded with _____ threads per inch.

11. The _____ micrometer consists of a basic micrometer mechanism with _____ rods of various lengths to provide a range of measurements.

12. A _____ depth gage can be used to measure the depth of a _____ or slot or the range of travel between two parts.

13. When it is necessary to make measurements smaller than 0.001 in it will be necessary to use a micrometer with a _____ scale.

14. A vernier scale is an _____ scale that divides the smallest graduation on the _____ scale into even smaller increments.

15. The vernier scale will always have one _____ division than an _____ length on the main scale.

16. The _____ gage is shaped like a T, with one fixed arm and one _____ arm.

17. To use the telescoping gage, the gage with the correct _____ must be chosen.

18. _____ gages are recommended to accurately measure holes smaller than _____ inch.

19. The _____ gage is used to determine the dimension of a gap or the _____ between two parts.

20. The radius and fillet gage can be used to check the _____ of a part being fabricated, or to check for _____ or other deformation of a part in use.

21. A _____ is an instrument for drawing or measuring angles.

22. Wrenches are sized by the _____ they fit and are made in _____ and _____ sizes.

23. The open-end wrench will make contact only on _____ faces of the bolt or nut.

24. It is essential that the open-end wrench be precisely made as clearance between the wrench and the _____ may result in the wrench _____ and rounding off the corners of the head.

25. When using open-end wrenches, it is better to _____ the wrench rather than to _____ it as there is less likelihood of _____.

26. The most effective type of wrench to use in turning a nut or the head of a bolt is the _____ wrench.

27. _____ wrenches are the most effective for use because they apply pressure to _____ points on the nut or bolt head.

28. Combination wrenches are manufactured with a _____ wrench on one end and an _____ wrench on the other end.

29. The adjustment mechanism of the adjustable wrench makes _____ of the wrench more likely.

30. When used the adjustable wrench should be turned in a direction so that the maximum stress is applied toward the _____ end of the _____ jaw.

31. Allen wrenches are made in a variety of sizes from _____ inch to _____ inch as measured across the flats.

32. The basic size of a socket set is determined by the size of the _____.

33. Metric-sized socket wrenches use standard _____ drivers.

34. The _____ is used to rotate the socket wrench in a area where only a small amount of handle movement is available.

35. The standard socket and the _____ socket are similar in design and use except for the amount of bolt clearance provided. Both are available as either a _____ point or _____ point socket.

36. A beam-type torque wrench has a _____ that moves across the indicating _____ in an amount proportional to the force exerted by the wrench.

37. A torsion-type torque wrench has the torque indicated by a small _____ attached to the wrench.

38. An adjustable toggle-type wrench is set at the desired torque value with a _____-type adjustment on the handle.

39. Torque wrenches must be _____ on a periodic basis.

40. A pipe wrench has jaws fitted with _____ hardened-steel teeth designed to grip _____ or _____.

41. An adjustable-hook _____ wrench is designed for use with large nuts having _____ cut in the periphery into which the hook may be inserted.

42. A pin-_____ spanner wrench is designed for use on nuts having holes drilled in the _____.

43. An adjustable pin-face spanner wrench is used to turn large nuts that are _____ flush with the part in which they are installed and has holes drilled in the _____ of the nut for the wrench.

44. When driving a screw, the _____ of the screwdriver blade should not exceed the _____ of the screwhead.

45. A recessed-cross design known as a _____ head provides a more _____ drive than is possible with a straight slot screwdriver and has become a standard for aircraft.

46. In order to get on a screw placed in such a restricted position, it is necessary to use an _____ screwdriver.

47. Combination pliers have jaws capable of _____ flat or round objects, have light _____ capability, and a _____ joint that makes it possible to enlarge the jaw width.

48. _____ pliers are similar in appearance and function to the adjustable slip-joint set but have _____ grooves making up the interlocking joints.

49. Adjustable lever-wrench pliers provide a powerful clamping force through the action of a _____ and _____ mechanism.

50. _____-cutting pliers are designed for cutting of wire, _____, nails, and other comparatively small soft-metal pins.

51. _____ pliers, also known as _____ pliers, are designed to reach into restricted areas.

52. _____ pliers are similar in function to needle-nose pliers but have wide and _____ jaws resembling the bill of a duck. The design provides for a greater _____ area than the needle-nose.

53. One method of classifying hammers is by the _____ of the _____ end.

54. To _____ a material, the tool must be _____ than the material to be cut.

55. The _____ consists of a steel tool with a _____ point.

56. The flat chisel has a wide _____ edge and is used for cutting _____ metal or thin _____ stock.

57. A hacksaw blade marked 1032 would be _____ inches long and have _____ teeth per inch.

58. The hacksaw blade should be installed in the frame with the teeth pointing _____ allowing cutting action to take place on the _____ movement of the saw.

59. Aviation snips are made in right-hand and left-hand designs, which refers to the _____ of the blades.

60. Aviation snips are designed so that the _____ jaw will push the metal out of the way.

61. Files consists of _____ metal shapes with a number of _____-like teeth cut into them.

62. The _____ of the file is the sharp pointed end and is designed for a _____.

63. The _____ of the file is one of the wide flat sides. The side opposite the face is called the _____.

64. The _____ file has a second series of teeth cut at an angle to the first. The first set of teeth, called the _____, is deeper than the second set, called the _____.

65. The curved tooth file has relatively large spaces between the _____, which allows the file to be used on _____ materials without clogging.

66. Six terms used to describe the coarseness of cut are (from most coarse to finest) _____, coarse, _____, second-cut, _____, and dead-smooth.

67. The _____ of a file refers to its general outline and cross section. Many files are _____, which means that they decrease in width and/or thickness from the heel to the point. Files that do not change in cross section are called _____ files.

68. The flat file has a _____ cross section that is _____ toward the point in both width and thickness.

69. The mill file may be _____ or _____ but has _____-cut teeth and is used where smooth finishes are desired.

70. A triangular file, also called a _____ file, is _____ and double-cut.

71. _____ consists of grasping the file at each end and pushing or pulling it across the work to produce a fine finish.

72. The tool used for boring holes is the _____, or _____, drill.

73. The _____ of a drill is the part designed to fit into the drilling machine and may be a plain cylinder in shape or be _____ for use in drill presses.

74. The body of a drill is the part between the point and shank and includes the spiral _____, the _____, and the _____.

75. Number-size drills are available in sizes from No. _____ (0.0135 in) to a No. _____ (0.2280 in).

76. Letter-size drills start with _____ (0.2340 in) and go to Z (_____ in).

77. Fractional-size drills start with 1/64 in (_____ in) and increase in _____-in increments to _____ in.

78. The _____ on the drill point vary depending upon the _____ of the material.

79. The drill point angle has an effect on the _____ of the cutting lips. For harder materials a _____ lip is desirable and therefore a _____ angle.

80. The lip _____ angle provides clearance between the cutting lip and the rest of the bit.

81. The angle and lip of each cutting lip must be _____; if not the result will be _____ or _____ holes.

82. Cutting speed is stated in terms of _____ (fpm).

83. The speed of drill bits are normally measured in terms of _____ (rpm).

84. The _____ of a drill bit refers to the _____ of the cutting lips into the work and is given in terms of _____ per revolution of the bit.

85. A general rule of thumb is that a _____ speed and _____ feed are used for hard materials.

86. A countersink is a pointed cutting tool designed to produce a _____ hole in metal or other materials to fit the head of a rivet or screw.

87. The _____ is a tool designed to bore a second hole that is larger than the first and _____ with it.

88. The _____ tap is used to start cutting threads in a hole.

89. The _____ tap is used when the hole is _____ and it is desired to cut threads nearer the _____ than is possible with a taper tap.

90. If it is required to cut threads all the way to the bottom of a hole, the _____ tap is used.

91. The center punch has a 90° _____ point and is used to make an indentation in metal to _____ the location of holes to be drilled and to make the drill _____ at the correct point.

92. The prick punch resembles the center punch in appearance except it has a _____ point. It is used during _____ work to precisely mark _____ locations.

93. The _____ punch has a long straight cylindrical end and is used to _____ and _____ various types of pins from shafts or other parts.

94. The scribe is used for _____ accurate lines on metal for _____ purposes but should _____ be used on pieces of metal that will be installed on the aircraft.

Chapter 11

Name _____

Date _____

APPLICATION QUESTIONS

1. What size wrench is used for an AN4 bolt?

   Answer: _____

2. What size wrench is used for nuts on 8-32 screws?

   Answer: _____

3. What number drill size is closest to a $\frac{5}{32}$-in fractional size?

   Answer: _____

4. Which fractional drill size is closest to the letter M drill?

   Answer: _____

5. Which letter drill and fraction drill are the same size?

   Answer: _____

6. You wish to install a screw that has a body diameter of 0.216 in. A clearance of at least 0.003 in is recommended. What size drill (number) are you going to use?

   Answer: _____

7. What is the recommended angle of lip clearance for drilling hard materials?

   Answer: _____

8. What is the recommended included angle of the drill point used for drilling plastics?

   Answer: _____

9. A material has a recommended cutting speed of 75 fpm. At what speed should you turn a letter F drill to achieve that speed?

   Answer: _____

10. A material has a recommended feed for the drill bit of 0.003 in per revolution. Using the speed found in Question 9, calculate how long it should take to drill through material $\frac{3}{4}$-in thick.

    Answer:_____

Chapter 11

REVIEW EXAM

Name _____

Date _____

Circle the letter of the best answer.

1. Identify the correct statement.
   a. An outside micrometer is limited to measuring diameters.
   b. Tools used on certificated aircraft must be an approved type.
   c. Dividers do not provide a reading when used as a measuring device.
   d. A propeller protractor will provide a reading in degrees or inches.

2. Which tool is used to measure the clearance between a surface plate and a surface being checked for flatness?
   a. Depth gage   c. Surface gage
   b. Thickness gage   d. Dial indicator

3. Which number represents the vernier scale graduation of a micrometer?
   a. 0.00001   b. 0.001   c. 0.0001   d. 0.01

4. Which tool is used to find the center of a shaft or other cylindrical work?
   a. Combination square   c. Surface gage
   b. Dial indicator   d. Micrometer caliper

5. If it is necessary to accurately measure the diameter of a hole approximately 1/4 in. in diameter, the mechanic should use a
   a. telescoping gage and read the measurement directly from the gage.
   b. telescoping gage and determine the size of the hole by taking a micrometer reading of the adjustable end of the telescoping gage.
   c. 0- to 1-in inside micrometer and read the measurement directly from the micrometer.
   d. small-hole gage and determine the size of the hole by taking a micrometer reading of the ball end of the gage.

6. What is generally used to set a divider to an exact dimension?
   a. Machinist scale   c. Surface gauge
   b. Thickness gage   d. Dial indicator

7. What tool is generally used to calibrate a micrometer or check its accuracy?
   a. Gage block   c. Dial indicator
   b. Surface gage   d. Machinist scale

8. What precision measuring tool is used for measuring crankpin and main bearing journals for out-of-round wear?
   a. Dial gage   c. V-blocks
   b. Micrometer caliper d. Depth gage

9. The side clearance of piston rings may be measured with a
   a. depth gage   c. thickness gage
   b. hole gage   d. telescopic gage

10. How can the dimensional inspection of a bearing (0.875 ± .003 in) in a rocker arm be accomplished?
    a. Depth gage and micrometer
    b. Thickness gage and push-fit arbor
    c. Thickness gage and V-blocks
    d. Telescoping gage and micrometer

11. Which tool can be used to determine piston pin out-of-round wear?
    a. Telescopic gage   c. Micrometer caliper
    b. Dividers   d. Dial indicator

12. Select the alternative that best describes the function(s) of the flute section of a twist drill.
    a. Allows lubrication to reach the drill body
    b. Straightens the drilling chips to avoid clogging the hole
    c. Forms the cutting edge of the drill point
    d. Maintains the proper cooling level of the drill

13. What should be the included angle of a twist drill for general purpose use?
    a. 118°   b. 90°   c. 65°   d. 45°

14. When drilling stainless steel, the drill used should have an included angle of
    a. 90° and turn at a high speed.
    b. 90° and turn at a low speed.
    c. 118° and turn at a high speed.
    d. 140° and turn at a low speed.

15. Which is correct concerning the use of a file?
    a. A file with an integral handle is referred to a safe-edge file.
    b. Apply pressure on the forward stroke only, except when filing very soft metals such as lead or aluminum.
    c. A smoother finish can be obtained by using a double-cut file than by using a single-cut file.
    d. the terms ''double-cut'' and ''second-cut'' have the same meaning in reference to files.

Chapter 12

1. A tube is defined as a _____ object, _____ in relation to its cross section with a uniform _____ thickness.

2. A _____ fluid line is not normally bent to shape or flared.

3. Semirigid fluid lines are _____ and _____ to shape and have a thin _____ in comparison to rigid lines.

4. Flexible fluid lines are made from _____ or _____ materials, and are usually called _____.

5. Pipe is a _____ fluid line made in standardized combinations of _____ diameter and _____ thickness numbers.

6. Pipes are joined by fittings utilizing _____ threads cut in the _____ of the pipe.

7. Although the use of pipe on aircraft is impractical because of _____, many components use pipe _____.

8. Tubes used for fluid lines are sized by the _____ diameter (OD) in inches and the _____ thickness.

9. Because of the thin wall thickness, _____ have been designed to allow tubes to be _____ to other tubes and to components.

10. Flared fittings require a _____° flare to be formed on the end of the tube.

11. Small sizes of tubing may have a _____ flare to provide a greater _____ of metal and more strength for the seal.

12. The basic components of a flared connection are the _____ nut, the _____ sleeve, and one of a number of fittings with a _____ to match the tube's flare.

13. A fitting with a long _____ and provisions for securing the fitting to a _____ are called _____ and/or bulkhead fittings.

14. Many aircraft components use _____ pipe threads for connections requiring a special fitting called a _____ nipple.

15. The use of pipe-to-AN fittings eliminates the need for _____ seals.

16. The outside diameter of the tube is expressed in _____ of an inch.

17. An AN819 fitting for a $\frac{1}{4}$-in tube would have a designation of _____ and for a $\frac{3}{4}$-in tube it would be _____.

18. High-pressure fluid lines made of material too hard to form flares use _____ fittings, made to _____ standards.

19. Many aircraft utilize swaged _____ to join tubes in areas where routine _____ are not required.

20. The advantages of the swaged-type tube fittings are: the original cost is _____ compared with that of standard AN or MS fittings, the installation takes _____ time, and substantial _____ is saved.

21. Hose assemblies are usually pressure tested at a pressure at least _____ the maximum _____ pressure.

22. The construction of a low-pressure hose, specification MIL-H-5593, consists of a synthetic rubber _____ tube with a braided _____ reinforcement and a synthetic _____ outer cover.

23. MIL-H-5593 hose is identified by _____ markings consisting of a linear stripe, called a _____ line.

24. The markings on a hose include a hose _____ code, the hose _____, and the quarter/year of _____.

25. MIL-H 8794 hose has a synthetic rubber tube with a layer of braided _____ and a layer of _____ steel braid for reinforcement with a rubber-impregnated braided _____ cover.

26. MIL-H-8794 hose is approved for aircraft hydraulic (mineral-base fluid), _____, _____, _____, and oil systems.

27. Many hoses are made of _____ (TFE or Teflon) and may be used for practically all _____ encountered on an airplane.

28. Medium-pressure Teflon hoses, specification MIL-H-_____, will have covers of a _____ steel braid.

29. Smaller sizes of high-pressure hose will have _____ layers of wire braid and sizes above $\frac{3}{4}$ in have a _____ wire braid reinforcement.

30. A hose is sized in accordance with the size of a tube with similar fluid-_____ capabilities and will use the same _____ number as that used for a comparable-sized tube.

31. Hose-end fittings may be of a permanent, factory-assembled design or may be designed to be _____ and _____ on new hose.

32. Reusable fittings consist of three parts: the _____, the _____, and the _____.

33. The permanent-type fitting requires _____ of the entire hose assembly.

34. Fire sleeves are installed on hose in areas where high _____ exist and _____ sleeves are used where the hose may rub against parts of the aircraft.

35. When a section of tubing must be replaced, it should be replaced with a tube of the identical _____, _____, and wall _____.

36. When a section of tubing is being replaced, the old section can be used as a _____.

37. Short straight sections of tubing between fixed parts of an aircraft should be avoided because of the danger of excessive stress when the tube _____ or _____ with temperature changes.

38. The wall thickness and the outside diameter govern the minimum permissible bend _____ for tubing, but it is advisable to make the bends as _____ as the installation will permit.

39. The radius of a bend is measured from the _____ surface of the tubing.

40. A small amount of flattening in bends is acceptable, but should not exceed an amount such that the _____ diameter of the flattened portion is less than _____ of the original outside diameter.

41. Soft tubing under _____ in diameter can be bent by hand without a bender.

42. The purpose of a flare on the end of a tube is to provide a _____ that is _____ between the sleeve and the body of a fitting and acts as a _____ providing a tight seal.

43. Before beginning the flare, the _____ and _____ should be slipped on the tubing.

44. Aluminum tubing with outside diameters less than _____ inch should be double flared.

45. A beaded tube is used to make a hose-to-tube connection by _____ the hose over the tube end and securing it with a _____.

46. An MS flareless fitting consists of a body or _____, a _____, and a _____.

47. The recommended procedure for installing a flareless fitting is to use a _____ tool to install the _____ on the tube.

48. While not essential to all fittings, _____ must be applied to some and is a good practice for others.

49. When applying a lubricant, it is important that none of the lubricant enter the _____ unless it is the _____ material as that used in the system.

50. Petroleum-base lubricant may not be used for the fittings of _____ systems.

51. For pipe threads, the lubricant must be of a type that is not _____ in the fluid being carried in the system.

52. A fitting must never be _____ into position.

53. Drawing tubing to a fitting by _____ the nut may cause the flare to be _____ off.

54. A common mistake made in tubing installation is to _____ the nuts in a pressure system, which may cause damage to the _____ and _____ and lead to a failure.

55. The basic principle of the reusable fitting is to _____ the hose between the _____ and the _____ with sufficient force to prevent a separation at the maximum pressure for which the hose is designed.

56. An end fitting for a high-pressure rubber hose has a hex-shaped socket with _____ on the edges of the flats and the _____ has a permanently attached _____-shaped surface for a wrench.

57. High-pressure hose must have the outer _____ removed from a length of the hose equal to the distance from the _____ of the socket to the _____ before installing the fitting.

58. After completing installation of end fittings, if the assembly is not installed on an aircraft, the _____ should be _____ to prevent contamination.

59. A leak caused by a loose fitting may be corrected by first _____ and _____ the fitting; if there is no sign of _____ to the fitting, tighten it to the proper torque.

60. A hose should be replaced if there is more than _____ broken wire per plait in the covering braid or more than _____ broken wires per lineal foot.

61. Hose that is reinforced with _____ steel wire braid is subject to corrosion, which may be detected by the _____ color on the surface.

62. Hose that is twisted, as indicated by the _____ line, can be corrected by loosening one fitting, _____ the hose, and retorquing the fitting.

63. If it is not possible to look inside the hose, a steel _____ slightly smaller than the ID of the hose should roll _____ through the tube from one end to the other.

64. A hose that is _____ to fit certain installations should not be _____, as undue stresses, wrinkling inside the hose, and other possible defects could result.

65. The installation of flexible hose assemblies requires that the hose be of sufficient _____ to provide about _____ to _____ percent slack.

66. Bends in the hose should not have a _____ less than _____ times the ID of the hose for normal installations.

67. Clamps used for beaded tube/hose connections should be tightened _____ tight plus one-quarter turn.

68. Synthetic rubber hose and hose assemblies should be stored in a _____, _____, dry area.

69. The following defects are not acceptable for metal lines:

    a. A cracked _____.

    b. Scratches or nicks greater in depth than _____ percent of the tube wall thickness or in the heel of a bend.

    c. A _____ of more than 20 percent of the tube diameter or in the heel of a bend.

70. Color codes for aircraft plumbing lines are established by _____.

Chapter 12

Name _____

Date _____

APPLICATION QUESTIONS

1. What is the outside diameter of $\frac{1}{2}$-in schedule 40 pipe?

   Answer: _____

2. What is the outside diameter of $\frac{1}{2}$-in schedule 80 pipe?

   Answer: _____

3. What is the inside diameter of $\frac{1}{2}$-in schedule 40 pipe?

   Answer: _____

4. What is the inside diameter of $\frac{1}{2}$-in schedule 80 pipe?

   Answer: _____

5. What percent reduction in the fluid-carrying capability (cross-sectional area) occurs if you change from schedule 40 to schedule 80 pipe?

   Answer: _____

6. What is the complete designation for an aluminum nut for a flared fitting that will fit a $\frac{5}{8}$-in OD line?

   Answer: _____

7. What is the complete designation for a 90° elbow to join two flared $\frac{3}{8}$-in OD tubes?

   Answer: _____

8. What is the number for a fitting that will join $\frac{1}{2}$-in and $\frac{3}{8}$-in flared tubes?

   Answer: _____

9. What is the designation for a 45° fitting that has $\frac{1}{4}$-in pipe thread on one end and an end for $\frac{1}{4}$-in flared tubing on the other?

   Answer: _____

10. What size of thread is used on -6 fittings?

    Answer: _____

Chapter 12

REVIEW EXAM

Name _____

Date _____

Circle the letter of the best answer.

1. Which coupling nut should be selected for use with $\frac{1}{2}$-in aluminum oil lines that are to be assembled using flared-tube ends and standard AN nuts, sleeves, and fittings?
   a. AN-818-2
   b. AN-818-5
   c. AN-818-8
   d. AN-818-12

2. High-pressure hydraulic tubing, which is damaged in a localized area to such extent that repair is necessary, may be repaired
   a. by cutting out the damaged area and utilizing a swaged tube fitting to join the tube ends.
   b. only by replacing the entire tubing using the same size and material as the original.
   c. by cutting out the damaged section of tubing and installing a short piece of high-pressure flexible hose with hose clamps.
   d. by cutting out the damaged section and soldering in a replacement section of tubing.

3. What is an advantage of a double flare on aluminum tubing?
   a. It is less concentric than a single flare.
   b. It has ease of construction.
   c. It is less resistant to the shearing effect of torque.
   d. It is more resistant to the shearing effect of torque.

4. A certain amount of slack must be left in a flexible hose during installation because when under pressure it
   a. contracts in length and diameter.
   b. expands in length and diameter.
   c. expands in length and contracts in diameter.
   d. contracts in length and expands in diameter.

5. What is the color of an AN steel flared-tube fitting?
   a. Black   b. Blue   c. Red   d. Green

6. If a flexible hydraulic hose equipped with swaged end fittings fails, which of the following repair procedures should be followed?
   a. Insert a nonmetallic hose liner, which is approved for use with the type of fluid contained in the system, and clamp firmly at both ends.
   b. Remove the hose fittings and reuse on a new flexible line of the correct length.
   c. Replace the hose with rigid tubing equipped with end fittings of the same type as those used in other parts of the system.
   d. Install a replacement hose of the proper length that has been factory equipped with swaged end fittings.

7. Select the correct statement in reference to flared fittings.
   a. AN fittings can be easily identified by the shoulder between the ends of the threads and the flare cone.
   b. All parts of the AN fitting assemblies are interchangeable with AC fitting assemblies with the exception of the sleeves.
   c. AC and AN fittings are identical except for the material from which they are made and the identifying color.
   d. AC fittings have generally replaced the older AN fittings.

8. Flexible lines must be installed
   a. where bends are necessary.
   b. only aft of the firewall.
   c. with just enough slack to make the connection.
   d. with 5 to 8 percent slack.

9. Soft aluminum tubing (1100, 3003, or 5052) may be bent by hand if the size is
   a. $\frac{5}{16}$ in or less.
   b. $\frac{5}{8}$ in or less.
   c. $\frac{7}{16}$ in or less.
   d. $\frac{1}{4}$ in or less.

10. Which of the following statements about MS (Military Standard) flareless fittings is correct?
    a. MS flareless fitting sleeves must not be preset on the line prior to final assembly.
    b. During installation, MS flareless fittings are normally tightened by turning the nut a specified amount after the sleeve and fitting sealing surface have made contact, rather than being torqued.
    c. MS flareless fittings should be lubricated prior to assembly.
    d. MS flareless fittings must be tightened to a specific torque.

11. What is the purpose of the lay line on flexible hose?
    a. Reflects hose twist
    b. Width of line corresponds to hose inside diameter
    c. Width of line corresponds to wall thickness
    d. Indicates the minimum bend radius for the hose

12. A scratch or nick in aluminum alloy tubing can be repaired by burnishing, provided the scratch or nick does not
    a. exceed 5 percent of the tube diameter.
    b. appear in the heel of a bend in the tube.
    c. exceed 20 percent of the wall thickness of the tube.
    d. exceed 10 percent of the tube diameter.

Chapter 13

STUDY QUESTIONS

1. In 1958, the Federal Aviation Act created the independent
   _____.

2. In 1967, the Federal Aviation Agency became the Federal Aviation _____ and was
   incorporated into the newly created Department of _____ (DOT).

3. Title VI _____ Regulation of Civil Aeronautics is the section of the FAA Act that is of most
   interest to aviation maintenance technicians.

4. Most safety standards and regulations are carried out by setting _____ standards and issuing
   _____ that the standards have been met.

5. An aircraft technician would be most directly involved with the Aircraft Maintenance Division of the Office of
   _____ (AWS).

6. The ten FAA _____ offices serve as an extension of the national headquarters and handle day-
   to-day problems that arise in the various geographic regions.

7. The technician's primary contact with the FAA will be with _____ inspectors assigned to the
   local _____ offices.

8. The FAA investigates most general aviation accidents on behalf of the NTSB, although the responsibility of
   determining _____ remains with the NTSB.

9. The Federal Aviation Regulations are published as Chapter _____ of the United States
   _____ of _____ Regulations.

10. Once a proposal has been developed for a new regulation or a revision, the public is notified by a Notice of
    _____ (NPRM).

11. A person seeking certification as a maintenance technician is expected to know the appropriate sections of three
    parts: _____, _____, and _____.

12. Part 91 establishes rules and procedures for _____ of all aircraft within the United States
    including the requirements for _____ the aircraft and maintaining it in an
    _____ condition.

13. Subpart E of Part 91 prescribes rules governing the maintenance, preventive maintenance, and alteration of U.S.-
    registered _____ aircraft operating within or _____ the United States.

14. The _____ or _____ of an aircraft is primarily responsible for
    maintaining that aircraft in an airworthy condition.

15. The owner or operator is responsible for seeing that _____ personnel have made appropriate
    entries in the _____ records releasing the aircraft for service.

16. Alteration refers to changing the _____ of the aircraft from that originally
    _____.

17. Major alteration means an alteration _____ listed in the aircraft, aircraft engine, or propeller _____ that might appreciably affect airworthiness.

18. A repair can be considered as the _____ of a defective condition.

19. Major repair means a repair that, if _____ done, might appreciably affect qualities affecting airworthiness, or one that is not done according to _____ practices or cannot be done by _____ operations.

20. Accepted practices are those procedures that are _____ in the industry.

21. Acceptable data refers to information that _____ be used as a basis for FAA approval for major repairs and alterations.

22. Approved data refers to data that has _____ been found to be _____ and thus approved by the FAA.

23. The holder of an aviation maintenance technician (mechanic) certificate may _____ maintenance, preventive maintenance, and alterations in accordance with the _____ and _____ set forth in Part 65.

24. Part 43 also allows persons working under the _____ of a certificated technician to _____ the maintenance, preventive maintenance, and alterations that his or her supervisor is _____ to perform.

25. The performance of a 100-h or annual _____ cannot be _____.

26. The holder of a pilot certificate issued under Part 61 may perform preventive maintenance on any aircraft _____ or _____ by that pilot that is _____ in air carrier service.

27. Section 43.5 states that an aircraft may not be returned to service after it has undergone maintenance until it has been approved for _____ to service by an authorized person and appropriate _____ has been completed.

28. Those authorized by Section 43.7 to approve the aircraft or component for return to service include the _____ of an aviation maintenance technician _____ as authorized in Part 65.

29. Section 43.9 provides the requirements for the _____ records and Section 43.11 provides requirements for _____ records.

30. The FAA issues an Aviation Maintenance Technician Certificate with two possible ratings: _____ (A) and _____ (P).

31. To be eligible for an aviation maintenance technician certificate, a person must be at least _____ years of age.

32. The applicant must _____ all the required tests, appropriate to the rating he or she seeks, within a period of _____ months.

33. Written examinations cover the _____ and _____ of aircraft appropriate to the rating sought and the applicable provisions of FAR Parts 43, 65, and 91.

34. After successfully completing the applicable written tests, the applicant will be eligible to demonstrate his or her skills through _____ and _____ examinations.

35. A temporary airman certificate is good for _____ days.

36. The FAA must be notified, in writing, within _____ days of any change of address. The details for this notification are provided in Section _____.

37. Each person who holds an aviation maintenance technician certificate shall present it for inspection upon the request of any member of the _____, _____, or of any federal, state, or local _____ enforcement officer.

38. A certificated aviation maintenance technician is not allowed to do major repairs to, or major alterations of _____, or any repair or alteration of _____.

39. A certificated aviation maintenance technician may _____ maintenance or alteration of an aircraft or appliance, or part thereof, and _____ the 100-h inspection on the portion of the aircraft for which he or she is rated.

40. A certificated aviation maintenance technician may _____ the maintenance or alteration of an aircraft or appliance, or a part thereof, for which he or she is rated _____ that he or she has satisfactorily performed the work at an _____ date.

41. A certificated aviation maintenance technician may _____ for return to service an airframe or powerplant for which he or she is rated after performing or supervising its maintenance provided that he or she has satisfactorily _____ the work at an _____ date.

42. An aviation maintenance technician may not exercise the privileges of his or her certificate and ratings unless he or she understands the _____ instructions of the _____.

43. Inspection Authorization is not a rating but an _____ to perform certain _____ functions.

44. Each Inspection Authorization expires on _____ of each year.

45. The inspection authorization will _____ be effective if the airframe and powerplant aviation maintenance technician certificate is _____ or revoked.

46. The holder of an Inspection Authorization may inspect and _____ for return to service any aircraft after a major repair or alteration to it in accordance with Part 43, if the work was done in _____ with technical data _____ by the FAA.

47. The holder of an Inspection Authorization may _____ an annual inspection or perform or _____ a progressive inspection.

48. To be eligible for a repairman certificate, a person must be _____ for a _____ job by a certificated repair station, commercial operator, or air carrier.

49. The FAA issues _____ certificates, production certificates, and _____ certificates for aircraft.

50. The type certificate is issued for a certain _____, or type, of aircraft, aircraft engine, or propeller.

51. A person seeking a type certificate for a product must make formal application in the manner prescribed in Part _____.

52. The holder of a type certificate for a product may, in the case of an aircraft, obtain an _____ certificate and obtain approval of _____ parts for that product.

53. Aircraft that are produced under a type certificate only are subject to individual inspection by the FAA for _____ with type design.

54. A normal-category aircraft is an airplane with a seating configuration, excluding pilot seats, of _____ or less, a maximum certificated takeoff weight of _____ lb or less, and intended for _____ operation.

55. A utility-category aircraft is an airplane with a seating configuration, excluding pilot seats, of _____ or less, a maximum certificated takeoff weight of _____ lb or less, and intended for _____ acrobatic operations.

56. An acrobatic-category aircraft is an airplane with a seating configuration, excluding pilot seats, of _____ or less, a maximum certificated takeoff weight of _____ pounds or less, intended for use without restriction.

57. A commuter-category aircraft is a _____-driven multiengine airplane with a seating configuration, excluding pilot seats, of _____ or less, a maximum certificated takeoff weight of _____ pounds or less, intended for nonacrobatic operations.

58. Transport-category aircraft applies to airplanes with more than _____ lb maximum certificated takeoff weight, except for those in _____ category.

59. An aircraft engine means an engine that is used or _____ to be used for _____ aircraft.

60. A propeller means a device for propelling an aircraft that has _____ on an engine-driven shaft and that, when _____, produces by its action on the air, a _____ approximately perpendicular to its plane of rotation.

61. A restricted-category type certificate will be issued for an aircraft that has been shown to have no feature or characteristic that makes it _____ when operated under the _____ prescribed for its intended use.

62. A person may apply for a production certificate if he or she holds a current _____ certificate, a license agreement, or an _____ for the product concerned.

63. The holder of a production certificate may obtain an _____ certificate without further showing, except that the Administrator may inspect the aircraft for _____ with the type design.

64. No person may operate a limited-category civil aircraft carrying persons or property for _____ or _____.

65. The FAA publishes the minimum standards for aircraft certification in several different parts depending upon the _____ of the aircraft.

66. Aircraft that had applications for type certificates prior to the early 1960s are certified under the _____ Regulation standards.

67. The four parts pertaining to aircraft (23, 25, 27, 29) are arranged in such a manner that the _____ number for a specific topic will be the _____ in all four parts.

68. The General subpart of an aircraft airworthiness standard lists the _____ for the part.

69. The Flight subpart of an aircraft airworthiness standard details the flight requirements that the aircraft must be able to _____ and/or maintain. The requirements for weight, center of gravity, and _____ handling are also in this subpart.

70. The Structure subpart of an aircraft airworthiness standard sets the minimum requirements for the various _____ that the structure must be able to withstand.

71. The Design and Construction subpart of an aircraft airworthiness standard contains factors and considerations to be used in _____ various parts or systems of the aircraft.

72. The Powerplant subpart of an aircraft airworthiness standard covers powerplant _____ and requires that the engine be _____ certificated under Part 33.

73. The Operating Limitations and information subpart of an aircraft airworthiness standard sets the standards for both the _____ and the _____ operating the aircraft.

74. Airworthiness Standards for type certification of propellers is covered in Part _____.

75. Part 39 prescribes requirements for _____ that apply to products when an unsafe condition exists.

76. No person may operate a product to which an airworthiness directive applies except in _____ with the _____ of the airworthiness directive.

77. Part 45 of the Federal Aviation Regulations prescribes the requirements for _____ and _____ marking of U.S.-registered aircraft.

78. Aircraft shall be identified by an _____ plate secured in such manner that it will not likely be defaced or removed during normal service, or lost or _____ in an accident.

79. The engine shall be identified by a fireproof _____ and _____.

80. A propeller blade or hub manufactured under a type or production certificate shall be identified by means of a plate, _____, _____, or other approved method of fireproof identification.

81. No person may _____, _____, or _____ the identification data on a certificated product without the approval of the Administrator.

82. A U.S.-registered aircraft cannot be operated unless the _____ and _____ marks are displayed in accordance with the provisions of subpart C of FAR 45.

83. Part 145 prescribes the requirement for the issuance of _____ certificates.

84. A certificated repair station located in the United States is called a _____ repair station and one located outside is known as a _____ repair station.

85. A repair station certificate gives an _____, rather than an individual, the _____ to perform maintenance, preventive maintenance, and alterations.

86. A _____ rating may be issued for a repair station that allows the performance of work _____ on a particular make or model of aircraft or even a specific component.

87. Each person who is directly in charge of the maintenance functions of a repair station must be appropriately _____ as a repairman or a mechanic under Part 65.

88. At the time application is made for a repair station certificate, the applicant must provide a manual containing the _____ and thereafter maintain it in current condition.

89. The repair station must give a copy of its manual to each of its _____ and _____ personnel and make it available to other personnel.

90. A certificated repair station may _____ for return to service any article for which it is _____ after maintenance or alteration.

91. If the repair station has an _____ rating it may perform the 100-h, annual or progressive _____.

92. The FAA requires those performing certain types of operations to comply with rules over and above those found in Part 91. These parts include _____, 125, _____, and _____.

93. These operators are required to develop, and have _____ by the FAA, a set of _____ specifications.

94. Aircraft with a passenger seating capacity of nine seats or less shall be maintained in accordance with the provisions of parts _____ and _____, and the operator must comply with the _____ recommended maintenance programs.

95. Aircraft with ten or more passenger seats will be maintained under a program required by Part _____, subpart J, and the operator must develop an approved _____ program.

96. The approved maintenance program must provide adequate organization, _____, and _____ to ensure that the aircraft are being maintained as provided in the certificate holder's manual.

97. In the event that a certificate holder contracts maintenance under a program required by Part 135, he or she shall ensure that the person performing the maintenance is doing so under the _____ of the regulations and the certificate holder's _____.

98. No certificate holder may operate an aircraft after maintenance, preventive maintenance, or alterations are performed unless an _____ is prepared, or an appropriate entry is made in the aircraft or logbook.

Chapter 13

Name _____

Date _____

REVIEW EXAM

Circle the letter of the best answer.

1. FAA Airworthiness Directives are issued to
   a. provide temporary maintenance procedures.
   b. prescribe airman privileges and limitations.
   c. present suggested maintenance procedures.
   d. correct an unsafe condition.

2. If an airworthy aircraft is sold, what is done with the Airworthiness Certificate?
   a. It must be endorsed by a certificated mechanic to indicate that the aircraft is still airworthy.
   b. It becomes invalid until the aircraft is reinspected and returned to service.
   c. It is declared void and a new certificate is issued upon application by the new owner.
   d. It is transferred with the aircraft.

3. The issuance of an Airworthiness Certificate is governed by
   a. FAR Part 23.   c. FAR Part 25.
   b. FAR Part 21.   d. FAR Part 39.

4. Which regulation provides information regarding instrument range markings for an airplane certificated in the normal category?
   a. FAR Part 21   c. FAR Part 91
   b. FAR Part 25   d. FAR Part 23

5. Which statement is true regarding the privileges of a certificated mechanic with a powerplant rating?
   a. He or she may perform the 100-h inspection required by the FARs on a powerplant or propeller or any component thereof, but may not release the same to service.
   b. He or she may perform the annual inspection required by the FARs on a powerplant or propeller or any component thereof, and may release the same to service.
   c. He or she may perform the annual inspection required by the FARs on airframe, powerplant, or propeller or any component thereof, and may release the same to service.
   d. He or she may perform the 100-h inspection required by the FARs on a powerplant or propeller or any component thereof, and may release the same to service.

6. Who has the authority to approve an aircraft for return to service after a 100-h inspection?
   a. A mechanic of any certificated repair station
   b. A certificated mechanic with an airframe rating
   c. A mechanic holding a repairman certificate
   d. A certificated mechanic with an airframe and powerplant rating

7. The 100-h inspection required by Federal Aviation Regulations for certain aircraft being operated for hire may be performed by
   a. persons working under the supervision of an appropriately rated mechanic, but the aircraft must be approved by the mechanic for return to service.
   b. appropriately rated mechanics only if they have an IA.
   c. appropriately rated mechanics and approved by them for return to service.
   d. appropriately rated mechanics, but the aircraft must be approved for return to service by a mechanic with an inspection authorization.

8. A person working under the supervision of a certificated mechanic with an airframe and powerplant rating is not authorized to perform
   a. repair of fabric covering involving an area greater than that required to repair two adjacent wing ribs.
   b. repair of a wing brace strut by welding.
   c. a 100-h inspection.
   d. repair of an engine mount by riveting.

9. Certificated mechanics, under their general certificate privileges, may
   a. perform minor repairs to instruments.
   b. perform 100-h inspection of instruments.
   c. perform minor alterations to instruments.
   d. not install instruments.

10. What part of the FARs prescribes the requirements for issuing mechanic certificates and associated ratings and the general operating rules for the holders of these certificates and ratings?
    a. FAR Part 43   c. FAR Part 1
    b. FAR Part 91   d. FAR Part 65

Chapter 14

1. The FAA issues _____ to inform the aviation community, in a systematic way, about nonregulatory material of interest.

2. Advisory Circulars are issued in a numbered-subject system corresponding to the subject areas of the
_____ .

3. The FAA program that provides for the collection, organization, analysis, and dissemination of information related to aircraft problems encountered during service is called the _____ Program.

4. General aviation service difficulties are generally reported to the FAA by maintenance personnel through the use of a _____ report.

5. When trends are detected in analyzing service difficulty information, they are made available to maintenance personnel through the FAA publication called General Aviation _____ .

6. Compliance with the recommendations made in Airworthiness Alerts is considered _____ .

7. Airworthiness Alerts are published monthly as Advisory Circular _____ .

8. The publications used by the FAA to notify aircraft owners of unsafe conditions that may exist in their aircraft are the _____ .

9. ADs are Federal Aviation Regulations and are published in the Federal Register as amendments to FAR Part _____ .

10. Airworthiness Directives are published in _____ books.

11. Airworthiness Directives contained in book _____ are not revised.

12. Each book of ADs is divided into the following four major subjects: _____ ,
_____ , _____ , and _____ .

13. The total collection of the ADs is referred to as the _____ of Airworthiness Directives, and is published every _____ years.

14. Airworthiness Directives contain two indexes. One is organized _____ by the manufacturer of the product and the second is a _____ listing of all AD notes from the oldest to the most current.

15. The indexes are updated every _____ months.

16. New and revised ADs are compiled by the FAA every _____ weeks and mailed out.

17. The six-digit AD number such as 92-10-05 identifies the year of issue as _____ .

18. When something of substance within the AD note has been changed, the AD is said to have been
_____ .

19. FAR Part 91.417 requires that the aircraft records contain the current status of applicable airworthiness directives including the following information for each: _____ , _____ , and the
_____ .

20. Type Certificate Data Sheets are issued for _____, _____, and _____.

21. Aircraft type-certificated under the old civil air regulations have _____ rather than Type Certificate Data Sheets.

22. Type Certificate Data Sheets and Specifications are issued in _____ volumes.

23. The statement ''Current weight and balance data report together with the list of equipment included in certificated empty weight and loading instructions when necessary must be provided for each aircraft at the time of original certification'' will always be found in _____ of the Data Sheet.

24. _____ of a Data Sheet pertains to the required placards for the aircraft and will include the following statement: ''The following placards must be displayed in front of and in clear view of the pilot.''

25. Part 21 of the Federal Aviation Regulations provides for the issuance of a _____ to persons who make major changes on a previously approved type design when the change is not so extensive as to require a new Type Certificate.

26. The manufacturer of an aircraft that applied for the issuance of a type certificate after January 28, 1981, must develop and furnish at least one set of complete _____ to the owner of each aircraft upon its delivery.

27. The section of the Instructions for Continued Airworthiness that sets forth each mandatory replacement time, structural inspection intervals, and related structural inspection procedures required for type certification is called the _____ section.

28. The medium utilized by manufacturers to communicate with owners and operators for such items as notification of design defects, possible modifications, or a change in approved maintenance practices is the issuance of _____.

29. Compliance with service bulletins is generally considered _____ with the general aviation operator.

30. A service bulletin can be made mandatory by incorporating it into an _____.

31. The technical publication that is most frequently utilized by the technician and contains the information necessary to check, service, troubleshoot, and repair the airplane and its associated systems is the _____ manual.

32. The _____ manual contains detailed step-by-step instructions covering work normally performed on a unit away from the aircraft.

33. The _____ contains descriptive information for the identification and repair of the aircraft's primary and secondary structure.

34. An _____ is designed to assist maintenance personnel in the ordering, storing, and issuing of aircraft parts.

35. The _____ manual provides information on all of the electrical and electronic circuits through the use of schematic diagrams.

36. The _____ manual contains information required to analyze and establish weight-and-balance procedures.

37. Information related to the installation, maintenance, and testing of products such as avionics, filters, instrumentation, and other components is commonly referred to as _____.

38. The Air Transport Association of America (A.T.A.) has developed a specification to establish a standard for the presentation of technical data by aircraft, engine, or component manufacturers that is referred to as A.T.A.

Specification _____.

39. The guidelines developed by the General Aviation Manufacturers Association for use in preparing manufacturer's maintenance data in a standardized format for general aviation aircraft is GAMA Specification

_____.

40. A piece of photographic film, measuring 4 by 6 in, that is capable of storing up to 288 pages of information is called

_____.

41. An FAA Approved _____ contains all the pertinent information

essential for proper operation of the airplane and in many cases is considered a _____ piece of equipment that must be kept on board the airplane.

42. The Federal Aviation Regulations permit the publication of a _____,
which provides for operation of an aircraft with certain items or components inoperative.

43. _____ are issued to supplement air carriers and air taxi operators and lists additional privileges and limitations that are not specifically covered by the regulations.

Chapter 14

Name _____

Date _____

APPLICATION QUESTIONS

1. Match the correct Airworthiness Directive Summary title with the appropriate definition.

   a. Small Aircraft, Book 1 _____   1. Contains ADs issued prior to January 1980 for small aircraft.

   b. Small Aircraft, Book 2 _____   2. Contains ADS for aircraft of 12 500 lb or more maximum certificated takeoff weight issued prior to 1980.

   c. Large Aircraft, Book I _____   3. Relates to large aircraft of more than 12 500 lb maximum certificated takeoff weight issued after January 1980.

   d. Large Aircraft, Book 2 _____   4. Contains ADs issued during and after January 1980 for rotorcraft.

2. The following is the compliance portion of an Airworthiness Directive: Compliance required as indicated, unless already accomplished.

   a. Aircraft with less than 500 h total time in service: Inspect in accordance with instructions below at 500 h total time, or within the next 50 h time in service after the effective date of this AD, and repeat after each subsequent 200 h in service.

   b. Aircraft with 500 h through 1000 h total time in service: Inspect in accordance with instructions below within the next 50 h time in service after the effective date of this AD, and repeat after each subsequent 200 h in service.

   c. Aircraft with more than 1000 h time in service: Inspect in accordance with instructions below within the next 25 h time in service after each subsequent 200 h in service.

   Given: An aircraft has a total time in service of 468 h. The Airworthiness Directive given was initially complied with at 454 h in service. How many additional h in service may be accumulated before the AD must again be

   complied with? _____

3. The following is the compliance portion of an Airworthiness Directive: Compliance required as indicated.

   (a) Within the next 25 h time in service, unless already accomplished within the last 75 h time in service:

      (i) Inspect the channel P/N 20749-0 and the two straps P/N 20749-5 and -6 in the area of the channel bend relief holes for cracks using a dye penetrant method or an approved equivalent inspection.

      (ii) Polish the rough edges of the bend relief holes.

   (b) Within 100 h time in service after the inspection specified in (a) above, visually inspect the channel and straps in the area of the channel relief holes for cracks, using a magnifying glass of at least five power or an approved equivalent inspection.

   (c) The inspection specified in (b) above shall be repeated at intervals not to exceed 100 h time in service from the last inspection.

   GIVEN: Aircraft total time 1856.5 h. Recording tach reading 976.0 h. Tach reading at last inspection 875.0 h. The logs indicated that paragraph (a), (i), (ii) of this airworthiness directive was complied with the last 100-h inspection.

   a. What part (paragraph[s]) must physically be conducted at this time? _____

   b. Must this AD be repeated (recurring)? _____

   c. If so, what would the total time be when the next inspection is due? _____

4. Match the appropriate volume of the Type Certificate Data Sheets with the correct definition.

a. Volume I _____   1. Rotorcraft, Gliders, and Balloons

b. Volume II _____   2. Large Multiengine Airplanes

c. Volume III _____   3. Single-Engine Airplanes

d. Volume IV _____   4. Aircraft Engines and Propellers

e. Volume V _____   5. Aircraft Listing and Aircraft Engine and Propellers Listing

f. Volume VI _____   6. Small Multiengine Airplanes

5. Many aircraft and engine specifications and some Type Certificate Data Sheets carry coded information to describe the general characteristics of the product. Using the following codes, describe the general characteristics of this aircraft and engine.

a. 4 P-CLM: _____

b. 6 HO A: _____

Chapter 14

Name _____

Date _____

Circle the letter of the best answer.

1. Which statement about Airworthiness Directives (ADs) is true?
   a. ADs can be complied with only by the manufacturer of the airframe, powerplant, or component involved.
   b. ADs are information bulletins issued by the airframe, powerplant, or component manufacturer.
   c. Compliance with an AD is not mandatory unless the aircraft affected is for hire.
   d. Compliance with an applicable AD is mandatory and must be recorded in the permanent maintenance records.

2. What is the maintenance recording responsibility of the person who complies with an Airworthiness Directive?
   a. Advise the aircraft owner/operator of the work performed.
   b. Make an entry in the maintenance record of that equipment.
   c. Advise the FAA district office of the work performed, by submitting an FAA Form 337.
   d. Record of entry is not required of the person performing the work. The aircraft owner/operator is responsible for recording maintenance.

3. FAA Airworthiness Directives
   a. are mandatory.
   b. present design changes.
   c. provide temporary maintenance procedures.
   d. provide suggested maintenance procedures.

4. Where are technical descriptions of certificated propellers found?
   a. Applicable Airworthiness Directives
   b. Aircraft Listings
   c. Aircraft Specifications
   d. Propeller type certificates

5. Which of the following is generally contained in Aircraft Specifications or Type Certificate Data Sheets?
   a. Empty weight of the aircraft
   b. Useful load of aircraft
   c. Payload of aircraft
   d. Control surface movements.

6. Placards required on an aircraft are specified in
   a. Advisory Circular 43.13-1A.
   b. the aircraft logbook.
   c. Federal Aviation Regulations under which the aircraft was type certificated.
   d. Aircraft Specifications or Type Certificate Data Sheets.

7. Technical information about older aircraft models, of which no more than 50 remain in service, can be found in the
   a. Aircraft Listing.
   b. Annual Summary of Deleted and Discontinued Aircraft Specifications.
   c. Alphabetical Index of Antique Aircraft.
   d. FAA Statistical Handbook of Civil Airplane Specifications.

8. What publication would a mechanic use to determine the fuel quantity and octane rating for a specific aircraft?
   a. Type Certificate Data Sheet
   b. Manufacturers' Parts Manual
   c. Summary of Supplemental Type Certificates
   d. Federal Aviation Regulations

9. FAA Airworthiness Directives are issued to
   a. provide temporary maintenance procedures.
   b. prescribe airman privileges and limitations.
   c. present suggested maintenance procedures.
   d. correct an unsafe condition.

10. For all aircraft type certificated prior to January 1, 1958, the CAA issued documents known as Aircraft Specifications, which contained technical information about the aircraft type. If an aircraft was type certificated May 7, 1959, the information that would formerly have been contained in the Aircraft Specifications will be in the appropriate
    a. Aircraft Operation Information Letters.
    b. Certificated Aircraft Bulletins.
    c. Type Certificate Data Sheets.
    d. Aviation Airworthiness Alerts.

11. Which of the following issues Airworthiness Directives?
    a. National Transportation Safety Board
    b. Air Transport Association
    c. Manufacturers
    d. Federal Aviation Administration

12. Which of the following is contained in a Type Certificate Data Sheet?
    a. Maximum fuel grade to be used
    b. All pertinent minimum weights
    c. Control surface adjustment points
    d. Location of the datum

13. Suitability for use of a specific propeller with a particular engine-airplane combination can be determined by reference to what informational source?
    a. Propeller Listing
    b. Propeller Specifications
    c. Aircraft Specifications or Type Certificate Data Sheet
    d. Alphabetical Index of Current Propeller Type Certificate Data Sheets, Specifications, and Listings

14. Advisory Circulars
    a. are issued by the manufacturer to correct unsafe conditions.
    b. are issued by the FAA as implementation guidelines.
    c. are issued by the FAA as federal law.
    d. have been replaced by Airworthiness Alerts.

15. Airworthiness Directives are amendments to FAR Part
    a. 39.
    b. 23.
    c. 43.
    d. 65.

16. An individual wishing to introduce an aircraft design change would apply for a(n)
    a. TSO.
    b. TC.
    c. STC.
    d. AD.

17. An Airworthiness Directive with the number 86-05-02 was issued
    a. July 1985.
    b. February 1986.
    c. March 1986.
    d. Not enough information is provided.

18. An Airworthiness Directive is issued when
    a. an aircraft accident occurs.
    b. an aircraft accident with fatalities occurs.
    c. an unsafe condition exists and is likely to exist in products of a similar design.
    d. a malfunction and defect report is received.

19. Airworthiness Directives can be issued as
    a. NPRMs.
    b. immediate adopted rules.
    c. emergency ADs.
    d. All the above

20. Airworthiness Alerts are issued by
    a. the FAA.
    b. the manufacturer.
    c. the ATA.
    d. GAMA.

21. The publication used to determine whether the correct engine is installed in an aircraft is a(n)
    a. Airworthiness Directive.
    b. Advisory Circular.
    c. Supplemental Type Certificate.
    d. Type Certificate Data Sheet.

22. Before a Minimum Equipment List can be obtained, the manufacturer must
    a. give its consent.
    b. re–Type Certificate the airplane.
    c. produce a master MEL.
    d. ask for exception to 91.171.

23. An aircraft owner flying for pleasure
    a. can ignore ADs in a solo flight.
    b. must comply with ADs when passengers are carried.
    c. must comply with all AD notes that apply to their aircraft.
    d. must comply only if aircraft is flown IFR.

24. What is issued by the aircraft manufacturer to correct design defects that may exist in an aircraft?
    a. Service Bulletins
    b. Airworthiness Directives
    c. Airworthiness Alerts
    d. Technical Standard Orders

25. The supplemental rules issued to air carrier and air taxi operators that are not specifically covered by the FARs are contained in their
    a. Minimum Equipment Lists.
    b. Approved Flight Manual.
    c. Approved Aircraft Information Package (AAIP).
    d. Operation Specifications.

26. General Aviation Airworthiness Alerts must be complied with by maintenance personnel
    a. during a 100-h or annual inspection.
    b. by the effective date contained in the alert.
    c. before further flight.
    d. never; they are voluntary.

27. A recurring AD would be one that
    a. is repetitive due to the nature of the condition.
    b. once complied with, would not be repeated.
    c. all ADs are recurring.
    d. All the above

28. An AD note on a Cessna 150 (1500 lb) that was issued in 1985 would be found in
    a. Small Aircraft, Book 1
    b. Small Aircraft, Book 2
    c. Large Aircraft, Book 1
    d. Large Aircraft, Book 2

29. The A.T.A. 100 Code is
    a. published monthly by the FAA.
    b. a standard for presenting technical data for large aircraft.
    c. a standard for presenting technical data for general aviation aircraft.
    d. All the above

30. Which of the following items may be type certificated?
    a. Aircraft
    b. Engines
    c. Propellers
    d. All the above

31. Malfunction and defect reports are compiled and sent out to the field in the form of
    a. Airworthiness Alerts.
    b. Service Bulletins.
    c. T.S.O.s
    d. Inspection Aids

Chapter 15

STUDY QUESTIONS

1. Spilled gasoline should be flooded with _____. It must never be swept with a _____.

2. Oil or grease on an _____ cylinder can cause an explosion.

3. Three requirements for sustaining a fire are:

   a. _____

   b. _____

   c. _____

4. Fire involving combustible liquids such as gasoline is a Class _____ fire.

5. Fire in which there is energized electrical equipment is a Class _____ fire.

6. Fire involving a flammable metal such as magnesium is a Class _____ fire.

7. Fire involving ordinary solid combustible materials such as paper or cloth is a Class _____ fire.

8. Certain materials such as rags soaked with oil or solvents are capable of generating sufficient heat to initiate a fire. This is called _____.

9. There are three basic ways to extinguish fires. They are

   a. _____

   b. _____

   c. _____

10. Class A fires respond best to _____-type extinguishers, which cool the fuel below combustion temperatures.

11. Class B fires respond to carbon dioxide (CO_2), halogenated hydrocarbons (halons), and dry chemicals, all of which displace the _____ in the air.

12. Class C fires involving electrical wiring, equipment, or current respond best to _____ extinguishers.

13. Class D fires respond to application of _____, which prevents oxidation and the resulting flame.

14. When working around an aircraft, all propellers should be treated as though the ignition switches are _____.

15. Three conditions are necessary for the starting of any internal-combustion engine. They are:

   a. _____

   b. _____

   c. _____

16. When starting a light-aircraft engine equipped with a float-type carburetor, the mixture control should be placed in the _____ position.

17. After an engine starts, the first instrument that should be checked is the _____ gage.

18. Before attempting to start a radial engine, the engine should be rotated several complete revolutions to eliminate the possibility of _____ caused by oil in the lower cylinders.

19. In hand propping an engine, the person who is turning the propeller should call out, "fuel _____, switch _____, throttle _____, brakes _____."

20. When, during the starting of a gas-turbine engine, the EGT exceeds the prescribed safe limit, the engine is said to have a _____ start.

21. If during starting a gas turbine engine, the engine fails to accelerate properly, it is said to have a _____ start.

22. In taxiing an aircraft the factors that influence the geometry of a turn are:

    a. _____

    b. _____

    c. _____

    d. _____

    e. _____

    f. _____

    g. _____

23. The disadvantage of using hemp rope for tying down aircraft is that it _____ when it becomes damp.

24. In order to prevent control surfaces from being damaged by wind when an aircraft is parked, it is recommended that a _____ be installed.

25. It is recommended that airplanes be parked with the nose headed _____ the wind.

26. When jacking aircraft, wing jacks are generally placed under the wing's main _____.

27. To ensure that the aircraft load is properly distributed at the jack point and to provide a convex bearing surface to mate with the concave jack stem a _____ is often used.

28. Aviation fuels are _____ to assist in preventing the fueling of aircraft with the wrong fuel.

29. Aircraft may be operated on automobile fuel only if the aircraft has been approved under the provisions of a _____.

30. Aircraft fuel filler openings must be marked to show the word _____, and the _____.

31. Gasoline flowing through a hose may build up a charge of _____.

32. Before starting the refueling operation, the nozzle of the fuel hose must be _____.

33. Two general types of aircraft fueling are the _____ method and _____ fueling.

Chapter 15

APPLICATION QUESTIONS

1. Match the shape of the symbol used to identify a fire extinguisher with the correct number for the class of fire for which the extinguisher is best suited.

   a. _____ Star   1. Class C

   b. _____ Circle   2. Class D

   c. _____ Triangle   3. Class B

   d. _____ Square   4. Class A

2. Match the correct number(s) for the fire extinguisher to the type of fire for which each is best suited. (More than one may be listed if appropriate.)

   a. _____ Class A fire   1. Halon

   b. _____ Class B fire   2. CO_2

   c. _____ Class C fire   3. Water

   d. _____ Class D fire   4. Dry-powder

3. Give the meaning of each of the light signals used by a control tower for aircraft operating on the field without radio contact with the tower.

   a. Flashing red light _____

   b. Steady red light _____

   c. Flashing white light _____

   d. Alternating red and green flashing light _____

4. Write beside each of the drawings the meaning of the signal used to direct an aircraft on the ground:

   a. _____

b. _____

c. _____

d. _____

e. _____

f. _____

g.

h. _____

i. _____

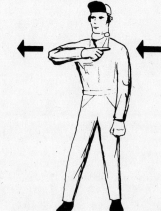

j. _____

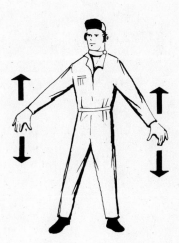

k. _____

5. List the correct aviation fuel color with the appropriate octane rating.

     Octane   Color

a. 80   _____

b. 100 LL   _____

c. 100   _____

d. 115   _____

e. Jet A   _____

Chapter 15

REVIEW EXAM

Name _____

Date _____

Circle the letter of the best answer.

1. When approaching the front of an idling turbojet engine, the hazard area extends forward of the engine approximately
   a. 35 ft.
   b. 5 ft.
   c. 15 ft.
   d. 25 ft.

2. The most satisfactory extinguishing agent for use in case of carburetor or intake fire is
   a. dry chemical.
   b. carbon tetrachloride.
   c. carbon dioxide.
   d. fine water spray.

3. Before starting a radial engine, the engine should be rotated several revolutions by hand to detect the possibility of
   a. compressive failure of the valve bodies.
   b. starter clutch damage.
   c. liquid lock.
   d. spark plug fouling.

4. The priming of a fuel-injected horizontally opposed engine is accomplished by placing the fuel control lever in which of the following?
   a. AUTO-LEAN position
   b. IDLE-CUTOFF position
   c. AUTO-RICH position
   d. FULL-RICH position

5. Which action would be required if the turbine inlet temperature exceeds the specified maximum during the starting sequence of a turboprop engine?
   a. Turn off the fuel and ignition switch, discontinue the start, and make an investigation.
   b. Advance the power lever and observe for excessive smoke; if present, discontinue the start.
   c. Continue the start since temperature will stabilize as soon as 5000 rpm is reached.
   d. Turn off the fuel and ignition switch, discontinue the start, then wait 5 min and initiate the starting sequence.

6. When towing an aircraft,
   a. discharge all hydraulic pressure to prevent accidental operation of the landing-gear retracting mechanism.
   b. all struts should be fully deflated.
   c. if the aircraft has a steerable nosewheel, the locking scissors should be set to full swivel.
   d. all nosewheel aircraft must be towed backwards.

7. When starting an aircraft engine equipped with a float-type carburetor, the carburetor mixture control should be placed in
   a. AUTO-LEAN position.
   b. IDLE-CUTOFF position.
   c. AUTO-RICH position.
   d. FULL-RICH position.

8. Gasoline spills on a hangar floor should be
   a. swept away with a dry broom.
   b. flushed away with water.
   c. put down a drain.
   d. left to evaporate.

9. Oil or grease can cause an explosion when combined with
   a. nitrogen.
   b. acetylene.
   c. shop air.
   d. oxygen.

10. Which of the hand signals below would you give if a taxiing aircraft were in danger of striking some object?
    a. A
    b. B
    c. C
    d. D

A B

C D

11. Which of the following indicators should be checked immediately after starting a reciprocating engine?
    a. Oil pressure
    b. Manifold pressure
    c. Tachometer
    d. Cylinder head temperature

12. The most appropriate type of fire extinguisher to use on a magnesium fire is
    a. water.
    b. halogenated hydrocarbon.
    c. CO_2.
    d. dry-powder.

13. When tying down an airplane in anticipation of a high wind, the control wheel should be in the full back position and the tail of the airplane
    a. pointed into the anticipated wind.
    b. pointed away from the anticipated wind.
    c. pointed across the anticipated wind.
    d. elevated into a level-flight attitude.

14. Grade 100-Low-Lead aviation gasoline is colored
    a. red.
    b. blue.
    c. green.
    d. purple.

15. Which of the following methods can be used to extinguish a fire?
    a. Cooling the fuel below its kindling point
    b. Excluding the oxygen supply
    c. Separating the fuel from the oxygen
    d. All the above

16. Extinguishers suitable for use on class B fires should be identified by
    a. a triangle.
    b. a square.
    c. a circle.
    d. a five-point star.

17. Jet A turbine fuel is colored
    a. red.
    b. blue.
    c. green.
    d. clear or straw.

18. Fuel filler openings *must* be marked with
    a. the tank capacity.
    b. the word "fuel" and the minimum grade.
    c. the usable amount.
    d. All the above

19. A turbine engine start that fails to accelerate properly is termed a
    a. hot start.
    b. hung start.
    c. slow start.
    d. normal start.

20. When taxiing an aircraft under the direction of light gun signals, a steady red light means
    a. OK to taxi.
    b. clear the runway.
    c. exercise extreme caution.
    d. stop.

Chapter 16

1. The inspection requirements for aircraft in various types of operation are stated in FAR
   _____.

2. For aircraft operating under FAR Part 91 the maximum interval between annual inspections is
   _____ months.

3. The procedures and scope of required aircraft inspections are set forth in Appendix _____ of FAR
   Part _____.

4. Certificated _____ maintenance technicians are authorized to
   perform a 100-hour inspection.

5. A certificated airframe and powerplant maintenance technician holding an _____
   issued by the FAA may perform an annual inspection.

6. An _____ inspection may be substituted for a 100-h inspection.

7. The 100-h inspection time limitation may be exceeded by not more than _____ hours, if necessary, to reach a
   place where the inspection can be performed.

8. To move an aircraft that is ''out of annual'' would require obtaining a _____
   from the local FAA office.

9. FAR _____ provides a list of rules for persons performing inspections.

10. A person performing an inspection is required to use a _____.

11. The complete airplane inspection requirements of both the 100-h and annual inspection can be satisfied with a
    _____ inspection.

12. A progressive inspection system requires that a person holding an _____
    supervise the inspection program.

13. The frequency and detail of a progressive inspection must provide for the complete inspection of the aircraft within
    each _____ calendar months.

14. Aircraft that are excluded from using 100-h, annual, and progressive inspections include
    _____ aircraft and multiengine _____ aircraft.

15. FAR Section 91.409 provides four options to the owner or operator of large or multiengine turbine aircraft in the selection of an inspection program. List the four options.

Option 1. _____

_____

_____

Option 2. _____

_____

_____

Option 3. _____

_____

Option 4. _____

_____

_____

16. Air carriers operating under FAR Part 121 are required to have a _____
maintenance program.

17. FAR Part 135 air taxi operators may use an _____ aircraft inspection program.

18. The inspection that is performed before each flight is called a _____ inspection.

19. In addition to the regularly scheduled inspections, many manufacturers provide for _____
inspections that are to be performed in the event that the aircraft is subjected to stresses outside of its normal operating environment.

20. In order to operate under instrument flight rules in controlled airspace, an airplane must have the altimeters and the static system inspected in accordance with FAR Part _____, Appendix _____, every _____ calendar months.

21. An altimeter and static test is usually performed by an appropriately rated repair station; however, airframe technicians may perform the test and inspection on the _____ pressure system.

22. Transponders are required to have an inspection every _____ calendar months in accordance with FAR _____, Appendix _____.

23. Each person performing an annual or 100-h inspection shall, before that inspection, _____ or _____ all necessary inspection plates, access doors, fairings, and cowlings.

24. A written list of defects located during the visual inspection of an aircraft should be recorded on a _____.

25. The principal purpose in performing an inspection is to determine if the aircraft is in _____ condition.

26. In order for an airplane to be declared airworthy it must meet two criteria: It must be in condition for _____ operation, and it must _____ to its Type Certificate Data Sheet.

27. In reviewing the aircraft paperwork, the aircraft registration and the _____ should be located on board the aircraft.

28. An aircraft that does not conform to its Type Certificate Data Sheet is considered to be _____.

29. Before an aircraft may be approved for return to service after an annual or 100-h inspection, FAR 43.15 requires that the _____ be operated.

30. Aircraft maintenance recordkeeping is a responsibility shared by the _____ and _____, with the ultimate responsibility assigned to the _____.

31. FAR _____ sets forth the requirements on retaining aircraft records.

32. Maintenance record items that are not considered part of the permanent records must be retained until the work is _____ by other work or for a period of _____ year after the work was performed.

33. Records that are considered permanent are kept for the _____ of the aircraft.

34. Records which are considered permanent are _____ with the aircraft if it is sold.

35. FAR _____ contains the requirements for inspection entries.

36. When a technician approves an aircraft for return to service after an inspection, an entry must be made in the maintenance records that includes the following items:

    a. _____
    _____

    b. _____
    _____

    c. _____
    _____

    d. _____
    _____

37. If an aircraft is disapproved for return to service because during the course of the inspection it was found to be unairworthy, a signed and dated list of the discrepancies must be provided to the _____.

38. FAR 43.9 governs the recording of aircraft maintenance and states that any mechanic who maintains, rebuilds, or alters an aircraft must make an entry containing the following items:

    a. _____
    _____

    b. _____
    _____

    c. _____
    _____

    d. _____
    _____

39. The main difference between an inspection record entry and a maintenance record entry is that maintenance entries are not required to include the total _____ of the aircraft.

40. Major repairs and alterations, in addition to being recorded in the maintenance record according to FAR 43.9, must also be recorded on FAA Form _____.

41. FAA-approved data that can be used for major repairs and major alterations may come from one of the following sources:

a. _____

b. _____

c. _____

d. _____

e. _____

f. _____

g. _____

h. _____

i. _____

j. _____

42. After completing an FAA Form 337, the original copy should be given to the _____ with the duplicate copy forwarded to the _____ District Office within _____ hours.

Chapter 16

Name _____

Date _____

APPLICATION QUESTIONS

1. What is the minimum inspection requirement on an individually owned Cessna 150 flown VFR by the owner for personal use?

   _____

2. The following inspections are recorded in an aircraft's maintenance records:

   Annual inspection, June 6, 1992, Total Time 363 h.
   100-h inspection, Aug. 8, 1992, Total Time 468 h.

   a. What is the date when the next annual inspection is due?

   _____

   b. What is the total time when the next 100-h inspection is due?

   _____

3. Indicate on the line preceding the following items if these items are considered part of the permanent aircraft records (P) or if they are temporary aircraft records (T).

   a. _____ Progressive inspections records

   b. _____ Copies of FAA Form 337 for each major alteration

   c. _____ 100-h inspections records

   d. _____ Propeller total time in service

   e. _____ Copies of FAA Form 337 for each major repair

   f. _____ Time since overhaul of all items requiring overhaul

   g. _____ Current status of AD notes and recurring action

   h. _____ Airframe total time in service

   i. _____ Identification of the current inspection program and times since last inspection

   j. _____ Minor alterations

   k. _____ Current status of life-limited parts of the airframe, engine, propeller, rotor, or appliance

   l. _____ Engine total time in service

   m. _____ Annual inspection records

Chapter 16

REVIEW EXAM

Name _____

Date _____

Circle the letter of the best answer.

1. According to FAR Part 43 what must be used in performing an inspection on an aircraft?
   a. A flashlight
   b. An inspection mirror
   c. A checklist
   d. A multimeter

2. An aircraft was not approved for return to service after an annual inspection and the owner wanted to fly the aircraft to another maintenance base. Which statement is correct?
   a. The owner must obtain a special flight permit.
   b. The aircraft must be repaired and approved prior to any flight.
   c. The aircraft may be flown to another maintenance base if the discrepancies are not "safety of flight" items.
   d. The owner must obtain a restricted category type certificate.

3. How long must the temporary maintenance records be retained?
   a. 6 months, unless sooner superseded by other work
   b. 9 months, unless sooner superseded by other work
   c. 12 months, unless sooner superseded by other work
   d. 24 months, unless sooner superseded by other work

4. The five items required in a maintenance record entry returning a minor repair to service are
   a. date, tach time, description of work, signature, and certificate number.
   b. date, total time, description of work, name, and certification number.
   c. total time, description of work, signature, and certificate number.
   d. date, description of work, a name, signature, and certificate number.

5. What is required to fly an aircraft after the annual inspection has expired to a place where the inspection can be performed?
   a. Nothing is needed as it can be exceeded by 5 hours.
   b. Owner's permission
   c. An A&P mechanic's permission
   d. A special flight or ferry permit from the FAA

6. After making a major repair to an aircraft engine that is to be returned to service, FAA Form 337, Major Repair and Alteration, must be prepared. How many copies are required and what is the disposition of the completed forms?
   a. Two; both copies for the FAA
   b. Two; one copy for the aircraft owner and one copy for the FAA
   c. Three; one copy for the aircraft owner and two copies for the FAA
   d. Three; one copy for the aircraft owner, one copy for the FAA, and one copy for the permanent records of the repairing agency or individual

7. When performing the operational check on the engine, which of the following RPM checks should be done?
   a. Idle and cruise rpm
   b. Static and cruise rpm
   c. Cruise and full-power rpm
   d. Idle and static rpm

8. How many hours may a 100-h inspection be exceeded if necessary to fly to a place where the inspection can be performed?
   a. 1 h
   b. 5 h
   c. 10 h
   d. 20 h

9. Which statement is correct when an aircraft has been disapproved for return to service after an annual inspection because of several items requiring minor repair?
   a. Only the person who performed the annual inspection may approve the aircraft for return to service.
   b. An appropriately rated person may repair the defects and approve the aircraft for return to service.
   c. An appropriately rated mechanic may repair the defect, but an IA must approve the aircraft for return to service.
   d. An authorized repair station may repair the defects, but an appropriately rated mechanic must approve the aircraft for return to service.

10. A twin engine turboprop aircraft may utilize which of the following inspection programs?
    a. 100 Hour/Annual Inspections
    b. Progressive Inspections
    c. Continuous Airworthiness Inspection
    d. Any of the above may be used.

11. The records of an annual inspection must be kept for
    a. 90 days.
    b. 24 calendar months.
    c. one year or until superseded.
    d. the life of the aircraft.

12. A progressive inspection schedule must provide for a complete inspection of the aircraft at least
    a. every 100 h.
    b. every 200 h.
    c. every 12 calendar months.
    d. every 24 calendar months.

13. An FAA Form 337 is used to record and document which of the following?
    a. Preventive and routine maintenance
    b. Major repairs and major alterations
    c. Minor repairs and minor alterations
    d. Airworthiness Directive compliance

14. Who must supervise a progressive inspection system on an aircraft?
    a. Owner or operator
    b. Authorized inspector
    c. A&P mechanic
    d. Any repair station

15. Where would you find the operating conditions that make a 100-h inspection mandatory?
    a. FAR 43
    b. AC 43.13-2A
    c. AC 65-19B
    d. FAR 91

16. Which of the following records are considered to be permanent?
    a. Major repairs
    b. Preventive maintenance
    c. Airworthiness Directive Compliance
    d. 100-h inspections

17. During an annual inspection, if a defect is found that makes the aircraft unairworthy, the person disapproving must
    a. submit a Malfunction or Defect Report.
    b. repair the defect before completion of the inspection.
    c. provide a written notice of the defect to the owner.
    d. remove the Airworthiness Certificate from the aircraft.

18. Before approving an aircraft for return to service following a 100-h inspection you are required to
    a. operate the engine and perform certain functional checks.
    b. notify the local FAA office.
    c. test-fly the aircraft.
    d. taxi the aircraft.

19. What appendix in FAR Part 43 covers the minimum inspection requirements on an aircraft?
    a. Appendix A
    b. Appendix B
    c. Appendix C
    d. Appendix D

20. Who is responsible for *making* the entry in the maintenance records after an annual, 100-h, or progressive inspection?
    a. The owner or operator of the aircraft
    b. The person approving or disapproving for return to service
    c. The pilot performing the test flight
    d. Any of the above

21. Which of the following aircraft would need a 100-h inspection?
    a. One in which the owner is giving flight instruction for hire
    b. One in which the owner is receiving flight instruction
    c. An aircraft on a progressive inspection schedule operated for hire
    d. All the above

22. Which of the following times are a required part of the maintenance records?
    a. Total time in service of the aircraft
    b. Total time in service of the engine
    c. Total time in service of the propeller
    d. All the above

23. An airplane on a progressive inspection program may also be required to have a(n)
    a. 100-h inspection.
    b. annual inspection.
    c. transponder inspection.
    d. All the above

24. Where would you find the recommended statement for recording the approval or disapproval for return to service of an aircraft after a 100-h or annual inspection?
    a. FAR 65
    b. FAR 91
    c. FAR 43
    d. FAR 43 Appendix D

25. An annual inspection required by Federal Aviation Regulations must be performed by
   a. a person working under the supervision of an appropriately rated mechanic, but the aircraft must be approved by the mechanic for return to service.
   b. an appropriately rated mechanic only if he or she has an inspection authorization.
   c. an A&P mechanic, but the aircraft must be approved for return to service by a mechanic with an inspection authorization.
   d. an A&P mechanic and approved by him or her for return to service.

26. Who can approve an aircraft for return to service after a 100-h inspection has been completed?
   a. Someone working under the supervision of an I.A.
   b. A&P mechanic
   c. Owner and operator
   d. Repairman

27. The six items required in a maintenance record entry approving a 100-h inspection for return to service are
   a. date, total time, type of inspection, certification statement, signature, and certificate number.
   b. date, tach time, certification statement, name, signature, and certificate number.
   c. date, total time, tach time, certification statement, name, and certificate number.
   d. date, tach time, type of inspection, signature, and certificate number.

28. Who is primarily responsible for having and maintaining the aircraft maintenance records?
   a. A&P mechanic performing the work on the aircraft
   b. Owner or operator of the aircraft
   c. FAA
   d. An authorized inspector

29. Which of the following is considered to be a part of the permanent maintenance records on an aircraft?
   a. Total time in service of the aircraft
   b. Record of all annual inspections
   c. Record of all service bulletins complied with
   d. Record of all 100-h inspections

30. On aircraft requiring a transponder inspection, how often is this inspection required?
   a. Once a year
   b. Once every 12 months
   c. Once every 24 calendar months
   d. Once every 12 calendar months

Answers

Chapter 1
STUDY QUESTIONS

1. digits
2. decimal / ten
3. whole / integers
4. addition
5. subtraction / minuend / subtrahend / difference
6. multiplicand / multiplier
7. product
8. division
9. numerator / denominator
10. proper fraction
11. mixed
12. equal
13. product / numerators / product / denominators
14. inverting / divisor / multiplying
15. decimal / tenths / hundredths / thousandths
16. round off
17. decimal / multiplicand / multiplier
18. dividing / quotient / dividend
19. decimal / common / lowest
20. decimal point
21. ratio
22. proportion
23. extremes / means
24. ratio / means / extremes
25. power / exponent
26. power / itself
27. square
28. factor
29. root / number
30. scientific notation
31. equation / equality
32. negative / positive / smaller / larger / larger
33. coefficient
34. literal
35. subtrahend / add
36. positive / negative
37. multiplications / divisions / additions
38. sign / changed
39. areas / volumes / distances
40. length / breadth / thickness / position
41. breadth / thickness / length
42. thickness / length / breadth
43. length / breadth / thickness
44. angle
45. circle / equidistant
46. polygon / straight lines
47. sides / angles / equal
48. triangle / 180°
49. Pythagorean theorem / hypotenuse / sum of the squares
50. square
51. trapezoid / two / two
52. square inches / square centimeters
53. length / breadth / depth / cubic / cubic
54. ratios / right
55. sine / cosine / tangent / cotangent / secant / cosecant
56. base / digit value / positional notation
57. base
58. binary
59. octal / eight
60. hexadecimal
61. broken-line / bar
62. circular / pie
63. continuous-line
64. nomograph

Chapter 1
APPLICATION QUESTIONS

Part 1:

1.	11	9.	12
2.	13	10.	70
3.	11	11.	79
4.	13	12.	98
5.	11	13.	98
6.	13	14.	119
7.	11	15.	142
8.	10		

Part 2:

1. 63	12. 532
2. 56	13. 1014
3. 54	14. 6231
4. 22	15. 396 576
5. 39	16. 691 164
6. 91	17. 20 989 644
7. 156	18. 43 547 166
8. 511	19. 29 421 700
9. 522	20. 29 287 458
10. 774	21. 38 720 220
11. 288	

Part 3:

1. 31	9. 17.00
2. 20	10. 9.42
3. 23	11. 1.87
4. 41	12. 1.08
5. 12	13. 2.94
6. 23	14. 1.62
7. 32	15. 2.41
8. 11.53	

Part 4:

1. 2	7. $\frac{7}{36}$
2. $2\frac{1}{16}$	8. $\frac{17}{90}$
3. $2\frac{7}{24}$	9. $\frac{41}{213}$
4. $1\frac{47}{168}$	10. $\frac{13}{30}$
5. $1\frac{19}{36}$	11. $\frac{7}{108}$
6. $1\frac{19}{48}$	12. $\frac{9}{49}$

Part 5:

1. 0.625	10. 871.2
2. 0.090	11. 10
3. 0.181	12. 392.46
4. 1/2	13. 20%
5. 3/4	14. 14%
6. 11/40	15. 30%
7. 19.5	16. 325
8. 100	17. 150
9. 29.24	18. 5634

Part 6:

1. 12	4. 10
2. 27	5. 30
3. 10	6. 2

Part 7:

1. 36	7. 41.57
2. 2744	8. 123
3. 70 225	9. 31.21
4. 1728	10. 36.25
5. 625	11. 36.60
6. 100 000 000	12. 27.58

Part 8:

1. 1.2345×10^8	6. 1.224×10^{-2}
2. $3.125\ 08 \times 10^{-1}$	7. 8 420 000 000
3. 3.1467×10^{-4}	8. 122.6
4. $1.73^{-}10^2$	9. 0.000 367 4
5. 3.25×10^5	10. 0.1344

Part 9:

1. a triangle with 2 equal angles
2. 60°
3. 10 in
4. 40 in^2
5. 35 in^2
6. 63.61 in^2
7. 14.96 gal.
8. 3.92 gal.
9. 314.16 in^3
10. 3.6
11. 4.95
12. 5
13. 0.8660
14. 0.6293
15. 0.771

Part 10:

1. 605 hp	6. 26 lb
2. 2000 rpm	7. 178 lb
3. 245 BMEP	8. 123 lb
4. 55 lb	9. 42 lb
5. 67 lb	10. 80 lb

Chapter 1
REVIEW EXAM

1. d	6. a
2. a	7. c
3. c	8. d
4. c	9. d
5. d	10. c

Chapter 2
STUDY QUESTIONS

1. metric system
2. knots
3. gravity
4. weight
5. mass
6. slug
7. density
8. specific gravity
9. hydrometer
10. speed
11. velocity
12. inertia
13. acceleration
14. terminal

15. friction
16. thrust
17. linear / angular
18. centrifugal / centripetal
19. work
20. energy
21. potential / kinetic
22. potential
23. kinetic
24. conservation of energy
25. mechanical advantage
26. lever / pulley / inclined plane / gears
27. fulcrum / effort /resistance
28. compound
29. increases
30. temperature
31. Fahrenheit / Celsius / Rankine / Kelvin
32. calorie
33. British thermal unit
34. 1 / 1
35. specific
36. fusion
37. evaporation
38. conduction / convection / radiation
39. radiation
40. conduction
41. convection
42. viscosity
43. density / height
44. force / pressure / area
45. solid / liquid / gas
46. inversely
47. direct proportion
48. general gas
49. vibration
50. frequency
51. hertz
52. amplitude
53. displacement
54. transverse / compressional
55. decibel

Chapter 2
APPLICATION QUESTIONS

1. a. 43.3
   b. 308
   c. 660
   d. 927
   e. 1390
   f. 194
2. a. 2
   b. 3
   c. 1
3. 30
4. 100
5. 15
6. 840

7. 40
8. 360
9. 3000
10. a. 25
    b. 10
    c. 1000
    d. 50
    e. 20
    f. 2000
    g. 25
    h. 7.5
11. a. 2
    b. 3
    c. 1

Chapter 2
REVIEW EXAM

1. c
2. b
3. d
4. d
5. c
6. d
7. c
8. d
9. a
10. c
11. d
12. b
13. d
14. a
15. d

Chapter 3
STUDY QUESTIONS

1. nitrogen / oxygen
2. 29.92 / 14.69
3. 1.98°C
4. directly
5. slug
6. density
7. less
8. decreases / increases
9. lift
10. airfoil
11. chord
12. camber
13. thickness
14. relative wind
15. angle of attack
16. stalling
17. square
18. directly
19. area
20. drag
21. skin friction
22. viscosity
23. boundary layer
24. laminar / turbulent
25. parasite
26. interference drag
27. induced
28. induced / parasite

29. resultant
30. lift
31. drag
32. center of pressure
33. 25
34. compressible
35. speed of sound
36. temperature
37. Mach number
38. a. subsonic
    b. transonic
    c. supersonic
    d. hypersonic
39. critical Mach number
40. oblique / normal / expansion
41. drag divergence
42. sonic booms

Chapter 3
APPLICATION QUESTIONS

1. a. 661.7
   b. 638.6
   c. 602.2
   d. 573.8
2. a. 2
   b. 6
   c. 4
   d. 3
   e. 1
   f. 5
3. a. 4
   b. 1
   c. 3
   d. 6
   e. 2
4. a. 2
   b. 3
   c. 1
   d. 4

Chapter 3
REVIEW EXAM

1. b	14. c
2. c	15. d
3. b	16. c
4. d	17. c
5. c	18. b
6. c	19. c
7. a	20. b
8. a	21. b
9. d	22. d
10. d	23. b
11. a	24. a
12. b	25. b
13. c	

Chapter 4
STUDY QUESTIONS

1. airfoil
2. airfoil profile
3. airfoil section
4. National Advisory Committee for Aeronautics / National Aeronautic and Space Administration / General Aviation—Whitcomb
5. Shape
6. a. Lift coefficient
   b. Drag coefficient
   c. Lift/drag ratio
   d. Center-of-pressure position
7. coefficient for lift
8. lift/drag ratio
9. CP coefficient
10. characteristic curves
11. wing area
12. aspect ratio
13. induced
14. tapered
15. plan, thickness
16. taper ratio
17. critical Mach number
18. mean aerodynamic chord
19. flap
20. camber
21. slot
22. slat
23. spoiler
24. angle of incidence
25. washout
26. washin
27. stall strips
28. vortex generators
29. wing fence
30. shock waves

Chapter 4
APPLICATION QUESTIONS

1. a. 3
   b. 2
   c. 1
2. a. 3
   b. 5
   c. 4
   d. 1
   e. 2
3. a. 3
   b. 2
   c. 1
4. 3.53
5. 0.3125:1
6. 1378.29 lb
7. 7833.57 lb
8. 17.0

Chapter 4
REVIEW EXAM

1. a		9. b
2. c		10. b
3. d		11. d
4. b		12. b
5. b		13. b
6. c		14. a
7. b		15. b
8. a		

Chapter 5
STUDY QUESTIONS

1. lift / weight / drag / thrust
2. center of gravity
3. center of pressure
4. weight
5. drag
6. load factor
7. normal / utility / acrobatic
8. wing loading
9. stability
10. static stability
11. positive
12. dynamic stability
13. longitudinal / lateral / vertical
14. longitudinal
15. lateral
16. vertical
17. roll / pitch / yaw
18. longitudinal
19. lateral
20. dihedral / sweepback
21. dihedral
22. directional
23. vertical fin
24. maneuverability
25. wings / vertical / horizontal
26. empennage
27. ailerons / elevators / rudder
28. flaps / trim tabs / spoilers / slats
29. ailerons
30. rudder
31. elevators
32. stabilator
33. trim tabs
34. controllable
35. servo
36. lower
37. gap
38. stagger
39. decalage
40. flying
41. centrifugal
42. coning
43. dissymetry of lift
44. blade flapping
45. Coriolis effect
46. forward / aft
47. hunting
48. gyroscopic precession
49. retreating
50. translational lift
51. opposite
52. collective-pitch
53. cyclic-pitch
54. tip-path plane
55. antitorque
56. antitorque pedals
57. aerodynamic
58. ground resonance

Chapter 5
APPLICATION QUESTIONS

1. a. 2 b. 4 c. 1 d. 3
2. a. lateral / pitch / elevator
   b. vertical / yaw / rudder
   c. longitudinal / roll / ailerons
3. a. 6 b. 4 c. 5 d. 3 e. 2 f. 1
4. a. 2 b. 1 c. 3

Chapter 5
REVIEW EXAM

1. a		22. b
2. a		23. c
3. a		24. a
4. c		25. b
5. b		26. b
6. b		27. c
7. c		28. b
8. c		29. b
9. b		30. a
10. d		31. a
11. b		32. a
12. a		33. d
13. d		34. d
14. a		35. b
15. a		36. a
16. d		37. a
17. d		38. d
18. d		39. d
19. c		40. c
20. c		41. d
21. a		42. a

Chapter 6
STUDY QUESTIONS

1. production / working
2. detail / assembly / installation
3. detail
4. assembly
5. pictorial / photograph

6. installation
7. block
8. schematic / functional / physical
9. wiring
10. logic / logic / symbols
11. perspective / converging
12. oblique / parallel / length
13. isometric
14. verticals / 30
15. front / top / right
16. wide / medium / narrow
17. medium / wide
18. invisible
19. center
20. alternate-position
21. narrow / dimension
22. cutting-plane / one / two
23. section
24. straight
25. sectional / cutting
26. detail / detail
27. dimensions
28. location
29. size
30. between
31. centers
32. size / drill
33. radius / arc
34. basic
35. limits / maximum / minimum
36. tolerance
37. allowance / mating parts
38. drawing number
39. number
40. opposite
41. station numbering
42. notes / duplicate
43. symbol
44. cast iron

Chapter 6
APPLICATION QUESTIONS

1. $2\frac{5}{32}$ in
2. $\frac{7}{8}$ in
3. $1\frac{3}{4}$ in
4. 0.664 in
5. 0.3130 in
6. $\frac{1}{2}$ in
7. $15\frac{37}{64}$ in
8. center
9. witness or extension
10. pictorial

Chapter 6
REVIEW EXAM

1. a	6. a
2. d	7. a
3. d	8. d
4. c	9. c
5. a	10. b

Chapter 7
STUDY QUESTIONS

1. gravitation
2. center of gravity
3. general law of the lever
4. moment
5. empty weight
6. maximum landing
7. weighing points
8. moment
9. station
10. undrainable oil
11. arm
12. + / −
13. pound-inches
14. empty-weight center of gravity
15. datum
16. Lemac
17. maximum gross weight
18. manufacturer
19. Type Certificate Data Sheet
20. usable
21. fleet
22. envelope
23. ramp
24. unusable
25. center of gravity range
26. leveling means
27. a. 6 b. 6.7 c. 7.5 d. 8.3 e. 170 f. 160
    g. 165
28. tare
29. main-wheel center line
30. subtracted
31. Temac
32. one-half
33. unusable
34. useful load
35. takeoff
36. empty / maximum
37. mean aerodynamic chord / datum
38. 25
39. wind
40. level
41. longitudinal / lateral
42. superseded
43. positive
44. negative
45. + / − / −

46. + / + / +
47. − / − / +
48. − / + / −
49. a. lowered structural safety
    b. reduced maneuverability
    c. increased take-off run
    d. lower angle and rate of climb
    e. lower ceiling
    f. increased fuel consumption
    g. overstressed tires
    h. increase in stalling speed
50. a. increased fuel consumption and power settings
    b. decreased stability
    c. development of dangerous spin characteristics
    d. increased oscillation tendency
    e. increased tendency to dive, especially with power off
    f. increased difficulty in raising the nose of the airplane when landing
    g. increased stresses on the nose wheel
51. a. increased danger of stall
    b. dangerous spin characteristics
    c. poor stability
    d. decreased flying speed and range
    e. poor landing characteristics
52. adverse loading
53. forward / forward
54. rearward / rearward
55. ballast
56. restricted

Chapter 7
APPLICATION QUESTIONS

1. a. A b. B c. A d. B e. B f. B g. B
   h. C i. B j. A
2. 35
3. 2.5
4. 33.68
5. 57.16
6. 151.365
7. 31.61
8. 1.62
9. 80.36
10. 151.1
11. 30.30
12. 12.73
13. a. 30 b. 64

Chapter 7
REVIEW EXAM

1. a   18. b
2. a   19. a
3. b   20. c
4. c   21. c
5. a   22. d
6. b   23. c
7. c   24. a
8. d   25. a
9. a   26. a
10. a   27. a
11. c   28. d
12. d   29. b
13. a   30. b
14. b   31. c
15. b   32. c
16. d   33. d
17. d   34. b

Chapter 8
STUDY QUESTIONS

1. plasticity
2. ductility
3. malleability
4. brittle
5. elastic limit
6. penetration
7. tearing
8. deformation
9. tension / compression / torsion
10. load
11. presses / crush
12. shear
13. three
14. twisting
15. normal
16. buckling / bending
17. yield
18. stress / strain
19. tensile / bearing / tear-out
20. strength/weight
21. thermal / electrical
22. thermal
23. solidification / space lattice
24. cubic / hexagonal
25. allotropic
26. slip / external
27. fine / coarse
28. harder / stronger
29. recrystallization / annealing
30. substitutional / solute / solvent
31. interstitial / solute / solvent
32. Type I / complete
33. stronger / harder
34. Type II / complete / limited

35. intermediate
36. original / cannot
37. chemical / electrolytic
38. strength / load cycles / reversals
39. structural
40. wrought
41. four / alloying element
42. copper / reduces
43. alloy / hardness
44. thermal
45. heat treating
46. pure aluminum / corrosion
47. 5052
48. 5056
49. 2117
50. 2024
51. 7075
52. iron
53. 0.20 / 0.30
54. carbon / brittleness
55. 4130
56. corrosion / toughness / high
57. austenitic / ferritic / martensitic
58. hardened / anneal
59. carbon
60. hardened
61. twice
62. lightest
63. corrosion
64. high / light / corrosion
65. strength / 56 percent
66. atmosphere / oxygen
67. 1950°F / burn
68. bronze / brass / beryllium
69. 1000 / 2200°F
70. thermosetting / thermoplastic
71. harden
72. softened / reformed
73. laying / mold
74. layers / plies
75. bonds / matrix
76. woven fabric
77. unidirectional / strength
78. both
79. Dupont / aramid
80. bonds / stresses
81. resin / the manufacturer
82. facings / core
83. sandwich / honeycomb
84. balsa / foam
85. solid / plywood / laminated
86. Sitka spruce
87. directly
88. greatest / parallel
89. across / longitudinal / between
90. laminated / same
91. solid / laminated
92. mahogany / birch

93. 9 lb-ft^2 / 160
94. 80 lb-in / 56 lb-in

Chapter 8
APPLICATION QUESTIONS

1. 39 690 lb
2. 1200 lb
3. 0.0083 / 25 000 psi
4. Material A
5. 908.1 lb / fastener shear
6. F
7. A
8. D
9. B
10. C
11. E
12. F
13. O
14. H
15. W
16. T4
17. T3
18. T6

Chapter 8
REVIEW EXAM

1. c
2. c
3. a
4. b
5. d
6. d
7. d
8. a
9. c
10. a
11. c
12. b
13. c
14. b
15. a

Chapter 9
STUDY QUESTIONS

1. letters / numbers
2. plastic / recrystallized
3. melting / mold
4. reduces / compressive / rollers
5. oxide / oxygen / surface
6. smooth / color
7. flow / compressive
8. extrusion
9. small
10. wires
11. strip / series
12. turning
13. opposing / offset / fracture
14. grain
15. cold / annealing
16. lattice
17. soluble
18. copper
19. precipitates / hardening

20. solid
21. quench / quickly
22. accelerated / aging
23. slow / intergranular
24. retarded / cold
25. heating / soak / slowly
26. carbon
27. hardened / tempered
28. carbon / austenite
29. ferrite / austenite
30. low / carbon
31. cementite / boundaries
32. ferrite / cementite / pearlite
33. pearlite / martensite
34. critical / rapidly
35. temper / reduce
36. heating / below
37. hardness
38. high / improved
39. reduces
40. heating / slowly
41. hardening / tough
42. carburizing / nitriding / cyaniding
43. solution / treated
44. less
45. some / not
46. strength
47. ball / width / impression
48. diamond
49. diamond / hard
50. detect / discontinuity
51. pocket / subsurface
52. heat / stress
53. clean / free
54. surface / subsurface
55. clearly / poorly
56. coil
57. through
58. magnetic
59. dye / seeps
60. surface / subsurface / surface
61. black / easier
62. magnetic / eddy
63. field / impedance
64. locate / sort / gage
65. sound waves
66. rays / photographic / shadows
67. corrosion / moisture
68. chemical activity
69. white / dark gray
70. more / more / more
71. heat treatment
72. highly / corrosive
73. slight
74. corrosion / prevent
75. wire / wool / abrasive
76. steel / steel / emery
77. anodized

78. replaced
79. active / critical
80. root mean square
81. film
82. sodium dichromate
83. cadmium / chrome / oxidation
84. electrolytically / corrosion
85. hardens / increases / dielectric

Chapter 9
APPLICATION QUESTIONS

1. H
2. B
3. D
4. G
5. F
6. A
7. H
8. E
9. J
10. A
11. 960 to 980°F
12. 315 to 325°F
13. T6
14. 30 min
15. 650°F
16. 1525 to 1575°F
17. 1450 to 1500°F
18. 1050°F
19. 63.0
20. 268
21. steel
22. 7075

Chapter 9
REVIEW EXAM

1. d	9. a
2. a	10. a
3. b	11. d
4. a	12. d
5. a	13. b
6. b	14. d
7. b	15. a
8. d	

Chapter 10
STUDY QUESTIONS

1. AN / MS
2. National Aerospace Standard
3. Society / Automotive Engineers
4. dimensions / details
5. quality / performance
6. aircraft / engines / propellers
7. screw / thread
8. 60°
9. major

10. root
11. half-way / major / minor
12. lead / one revolution
13. fine / coarse
14. $\frac{1}{4}$-in / screw
15. smallest / largest
16. #10
17. loose / tight
18. bolts / screws
19. nut / grip
20. diameter / length
21. tension / shear
22. diameter / sixteenths
23. castellated / cotter pin
24. alloy / corrosion-resistant
25. asterisk / two / one
26. $\frac{3}{16}$-in / $\frac{1}{4}$-in / primary
27. light drive
28. engine / crankcase
29. shear
30. bolt / clamping
31. safety / cotter
32. friction
33. cotter pin
34. plain / left / right
35. insert / distorted
36. 1032
37. prohibit / rotation / addition
38. crushed / grip / locking
39. wood / wood
40. twisted / friction
41. twisted / flattened
42. castellated / drilled
43. cadmium / corrosion-resistant
44. threaded
45. coarse / 2 / AN3
46. recessed
47. 100° / countersunk
48. truss / clamping
49. area / tension
50. deep / diameter
51. steel / grip
52. sheet-metal / nonstructural
53. sharp / blunt
54. ends / arms
55. shear / upsetting
56. diameter / tight
57. head marking
58. heat-treated / immediately
59. 2117
60. magnesium
61. diameter / length
62. rivets
63. critical / fill
64. collar / stem
65. bulbed / clamping
66. installation
67. rivet / threads / thin

68. shear
69. pin / swaged
70. pin / hole size
71. pull / stump
72. threaded
73. Dzus / Camloc / Airloc
74. junction / slipped
75. tension
76. barrel / right / left
77. groove
78. three
79. occupied / approved
80. nameplate / identification

Chapter 10
APPLICATION QUESTIONS

1. AN5-12A
2. AN365-524
3. AN4C10
4. AN310-4 / AN960-416
5. AN175
6. AN381-3-12
7. AN380-2-2
8. AN25-12
9. AN501
10. MS20470DD5-14

Chapter 10
REVIEW EXAM

1. b
2. d
3. c
4. a
5. d
6. b
7. b
8. b
9. b
10. a
11. b
12. d
13. b
14. d
15. d

Chapter 11
STUDY QUESTIONS

1. transferring / drawing
2. scale / graduations
3. value / graduations
4. gage / rule / dimension
5. straight / transfer / scale
6. slide / fixed
7. inside / outside
8. hub / spindle / thimble
9. range / one
10. 0.001 / 40
11. inside / extension
12. micrometer / hole
13. vernier
14. auxiliary / main
15. more / equal
16. telescoping / telescoping

17. size range
18. small-hole / $\frac{1}{2}$
19. thickness / clearance
20. radius / stretch
21. protractor
22. hardware / fractional / metric
23. two
24. head / slipping
25. pull / push / slipping
26. box-end
27. box-end / six
28. box-end / open-end
29. slippage
30. inner / fixed
31. 0.028 / $\frac{3}{4}$
32. drive
33. fractional-sized
34. ratchet handle
35. deep / six / twelve
36. pointer / scale
37. dial gage
38. micrometer
39. calibrated
40. sharp / pipes / rods
41. spanner / notches
42. hook / periphery
43. recessed / face
44. width / diameter
45. Phillips / positive
46. offset
47. gripping / cutting / slip
48. channel-lock / curved
49. cam / lever
50. diagonal / cotter / pins
51. needle-nose / long-nose
52. duck-bill / flat / gripping
53. shape / peen
54. cut / harder
55. chisel / hardened
56. cutting / sheet / bar
57. 10 / 32
58. forward / forward
59. relative position
60. lower
61. hardened / chisel
62. tang / handle
63. face / back
64. double-cut / overcut / upcut
65. teeth / soft
66. rough / bastard / smooth
67. shape / tapered / blunt
68. rectangular / slightly tapered
69. tapered / blunt / single
70. three-square / tapered
71. drawfiling
72. spiral / twist
73. shank / tapered
74. flutes / lands / margin

75. 80 / 1
76. A / 0.4130
77. 0.0156 / 1/64 / 1
78. angles / hardness
79. length / shorter / blunter
80. clearance
81. equal / oversized / distorted
82. feet per minute
83. revolutions per minute
84. feed / advancement / inches
85. slow / heavy
86. conical-shaped
87. counterbore / concentric
88. taper
89. plug / blind / bottom
90. bottoming
91. conical / mark / start
92. sharper / layout / center
93. pin / drive / remove
94. marking / layout / not

Chapter 11
APPLICATION QUESTIONS

1. $\frac{7}{16}$
2. $\frac{11}{32}$
3. #22
4. $\frac{19}{64}$
5. E and $\frac{1}{4}$-in
6. #2 (0.221)
7. 8°
8. 90°
9. 1167 rpm
10. 0.214 min or about 13 s

Chapter 11
REVIEW EXAM

1. c	9. c
2. b	10. d
3. c	11. c
4. a	12. c
5. d	13. a
6. a	14. d
7. a	15. b
8. b	

Chapter 12
STUDY QUESTIONS

1. hollow / long / wall
2. rigid
3. bent / formed / wall
4. rubber / synthetic / hoses
5. rigid / outside / wall
6. tapered / wall
7. weight / threads
8. outside / wall
9. fittings / connected

10. 37
11. double / thickness
12. AN818 / AN819 / cone
13. body / bulkhead / universal
14. internal / pipe-to-AN
15. rubber
16. sixteenths
17. AN819-4 / AN819-12
18. flareless / MS
19. fittings / disconnections
20. low / less / weight
21. twice / operating
22. inner / cotton / rubber
23. yellow / lay
24. manufacturer's / size / manufacture
25. cotton / stainless / cotton
26. pneumatic / coolant / fuel
27. tetrafluoroethylene / fluids
28. 27267 / stainless
29. two / triple
30. carrying / dash
31. removed / reused
32. socket / nipple / sleeve
33. replacement
34. temperatures / abrasion
35. material / diameter / thickness
36. pattern
37. expands / contracts
38. radius / large
39. inner
40. small / 75 percent
41. $\frac{1}{4}$ in.
42. flange / gripped / gasket
43. sleeve / nut
44. $\frac{3}{8}$
45. sliding / hose / clamp
46. fitting / sleeve / nut
47. presetting / sleeve
48. lubrication
49. tubing / same
50. oxygen
51. soluble
52. forced
53. tightening / sheared
54. overtighten / tubing / fittings
55. clamp / socket / nipple
56. notches / nipple / hex
57. cover / end / notches
58. ends / capped
59. loosening / inspecting / damage
60. one / six
61. carbon / rust
62. lay / straightening
63. ball / freely
64. preformed / straightened
65. length / 5 / 8
66. radius / 12
67. finger
68. dark / cool
69. flare / 10 / dent
70. AND10375

Chapter 12
APPLICATION QUESTIONS

1. 0.840 in
2. 0.840 in
3. 0.622 in
4. 0.546 in
5. 22.7 percent
6. AN818D10
7. AN821-6
8. AN919-12
9. AN823-4-4
10. 9/16-18

Chapter 12
REVIEW EXAM

1. c
2. a
3. d
4. d
5. a
6. d
7. a
8. d
9. d
10. b
11. a
12. b

Chapter 13
STUDY QUESTIONS

1. Federal Aviation Agency
2. Administration / Transportation
3. Safety
4. minimum / certification
5. Airworthiness
6. regional
7. airworthiness / district
8. probable cause
9. 14 / Code / Federal
10. Proposed Rule Making
11. 43 / 65 / 91
12. operation / inspecting / airworthy
13. civil / outside
14. owner / operator
15. maintenance / maintenance
16. design / certificated
17. not / specification
18. correction
19. improperly / accepted / elementary
20. widespread
21. may
22. previously / acceptable
23. perform / privileges / limitations
24. supervision / perform / authorized
25. inspection / supervised
26. owned / operated / not used
27. return / paperwork
28. holder / certificate
29. maintenance / inspection
30. Airframe / Powerplant
31. 18
32. pass / 24

33. construction / maintenance
34. oral / practical
35. 120
36. 30 / 65.21
37. FAA / NTSB / law
38. propellers / instruments
39. perform / perform
40. supervise / provided / earlier
41. approve / performed / earlier
42. current / manufacturer
43. authorization / inspection
44. March 31
45. not / suspended
46. approve / accordance / approved
47. perform / supervise
48. employed / specific
49. type / airworthiness
50. design
51. 21
52. airworthiness / replacement
53. conformity
54. nine / 12 500 / nonacrobatic
55. nine / 12 500 / limited
56. nine / 12 500
57. propeller / 19 / 19 000
58. 12 500 / commuter
59. intended / propelling
60. blades / rotated / thrust
61. unsafe / limitations
62. type / STC
63. airworthiness / conformity
64. compensation / hire
65. use
66. Civil Air
67. section / same
68. applicability
69. perform / ground
70. loads
71. designing
72. installation / type
73. equipment / personnel
74. 35
75. airworthiness directives
76. accordance / requirements
77. nationality / registration
78. identification / destroyed
79. plate / markings
80. stamping / etching
81. remove / replace / change
82. nationality / registration
83. repair station
84. domestic / foreign
85. agency / authorization
86. limited / only
87. certificated
88. inspection procedures
89. supervisory / inspection
90. approve / rated

91. airframe / inspections
92. 121 / 127 / 135
93. approved / operating
94. 43 / 91 / manufacturer's
95. 135 / maintenance
96. procedure / instruction
97. provisions / manual
98. airworthiness release

Chapter 13
REVIEW EXAM

1. d		6. d	
2. d		7. c	
3. b		8. c	
4. d		9. b	
5. d		10. d	

Chapter 14
STUDY QUESTIONS

1. Advisory Circulars
2. Federal Aviation Regulations
3. Service Difficulty
4. Malfunction and Defect
5. Airworthiness Alerts
6. voluntary
7. 43-16
8. Airworthiness Directives
9. 39
10. four
11. one
12. aircraft / engines / propellers / appliances
13. summary / two
14. alphabetically / numerical
15. six
16. two
17. 1992
18. revised
19. AD number / method of compliance / revision date
20. aircraft / aircraft engines / propellers
21. Aircraft Specifications
22. six
23. Note 1
24. Note 2
25. Supplemental Type Certificate
26. Instructions for Continued Airworthiness
27. Airworthiness Limitations
28. service bulletins
29. voluntary
30. Airworthiness Directive
31. maintenance
32. overhaul
33. structural repair manual
34. illustrated parts catalog
35. wiring diagram
36. weight-and-balance
37. vendor data

38. No. 100
39. No. 2
40. microfiche
41. Flight Manual / required
42. Minimum Equipment List
43. Operation Specifications

Chapter 14
APPLICATION QUESTIONS

1. a. 1 b. 4 c. 2 d. 3
2. 200 h
3. a. b b. yes c. 1956.5
4. a. 3 b. 6 c. 2 d. 1 e. 4 f. 5
5. a. 4 place aircraft, closed cockpit, land, monoplane
   b. 6 cylinder engine, horizontally opposed, air-cooled

Chapter 14
REVIEW EXAM

1. d	17. c
2. b	18. c
3. a	19. d
4. d	20. a
5. d	21. d
6. d	22. c
7. a	23. c
8. a	24. a
9. d	25. d
10. c	26. d
11. d	27. a
12. d	28. b
13. c	29. b
14. b	30. d
15. a	31. a
16. c	

Chapter 15
STUDY QUESTIONS

1. water / dry broom
2. oxygen
3. a. fuel b. oxygen c. heat
4. B
5. C
6. D
7. A
8. spontaneous combustion
9. a. cooling the fuel below its kindling point
   b. excluding the oxygen supply
   c. separating the fuel supply
10. water
11. oxygen
12. carbon dioxide
13. dry powder
14. ON

15. a. the presence of fuel in the combustion chamber
    b. a source of ignition
    c. a method for rotating the engine to start
16. Full Rich
17. oil-pressure
18. liquid lock
19. on / off / closed / on
20. hot
21. false (hung)
22. a. degree of nose wheel steering angle
    b. engine power settings
    c. center-of-gravity location
    d. gross weight
    e. pavement surface conditions
    f. ground speed
    g. amount of differential braking
23. shrinks
24. control (gust) lock
25. into
26. spar
27. jack pad
28. color-coded
29. Supplemental Type Certificate
30. fuel / minimum fuel grade
31. static electricity
32. grounded
33. overwing / pressure

Chapter 15
APPLICATION QUESTIONS

1. a. 2 b. 1 c. 4 d. 3
2. a. 3 b. 1, 2 c. 1, 2 d. 4
3. a. taxi clear of the runway b. stop c. return to starting point d. taxi with extreme caution
4. a. all clear b. start engines c. stop d. come ahead e. pull chocks f. left turn g. right turn h. insert chocks i. emergency stop j. cut engines k. slow down
5. a. red b. blue c. green d. purple e. clear or straw colored

Chapter 15
REVIEW EXAM

1. d	11. a
2. c	12. d
3. c	13. b
4. d	14. b
5. a	15. d
6. c	16. b
7. d	17. d
8. b	18. b
9. d	19. b
10. c	20. d

Chapter 16
STUDY QUESTIONS

1. 91.409
2. 12 calendar
3. D / 43
4. airframe and powerplant
5. inspection authorization
6. annual
7. 10
8. special airworthiness certificate
9. 43.15
10. checklist
11. progressive
12. inspection authorization
13. 12
14. large / turbine
15. Option 1. A continuous airworthiness inspection program that is a part of a continuous airworthiness maintenance program currently in use by a person holding a certificate issued under FAR Part 121
    Option 2. An approved aircraft inspection program currently in use by a person holding an air taxi certificate under FAR Part 135
    Option 3. A current inspection program recommended by the manufacturer
    Option 4. Any other inspection program established by the registered owner or operator of the airplane and approved by the Administrator
16. continuous airworthiness
17. approved
18. preflight
19. special
20. 43 / E / 24
21. static
22. 24 / 43 / F
23. remove / open
24. discrepancy report
25. airworthy
26. safe / conform
27. airworthiness certificate
28. unairworthy
29. engines
30. owner / maintenance technician / owner
31. 91.417
32. superseded / 1
33. life
34. transferred
35. 43.11

36. a. The type of inspection and a brief description of the extent of the inspection
    b. The date of the inspection and aircraft total time in service
    c. The signature, the certificate number, and kind of certificate held by the person approving or disapproving returning the aircraft to service
    d. If the aircraft is found to be airworthy and approved for return to service, the following or a similarly worded statement: ''I certify that this aircraft has been inspected in accordance with (insert type) inspection and was determined to be in airworthy condition.''
37. owner
38. a. A description of the work or some reference to data acceptable to the FAA
    b. The date the work was completed
    c. The mechanic's name
    d. If it is approved for return to service, the signature and certificate number of the approving mechanic
39. time
40. 337
41. a. Type Certificate Data Sheets
    b. Aircraft Specifications
    c. Supplemental Type Certificates (STCs)
    d. Airworthiness Directives
    e. FAA Field Approval
    f. Manufacturer's FAA Approved Data
    g. Designated Engineering Representative (DER) Approved Data
    h. Designated Alteration Station (DAS) Approved Data
    i. Appliance Manufacturer's Manuals
    j. AC 43.13-1A may be used as approved data when it is appropriate to the product being repaired.
42. owner / FAA / 48

Chapter 16
APPLICATION QUESTIONS

1. annual inspection
2. a. June 30, 1993   b. 563 hours
3. a. T b. P c. T d. T e. T f. P g. P
   h. P i. T j. T k. P l. P m. T

Chapter 16
REVIEW EXAM

1. c
2. a
3. c
4. d
5. d
6. b
7. d
8. c
9. b
10. c
11. c
12. c
13. b
14. b
15. d

16. c
17. c
18. a
19. d
20. b
21. a
22. d
23. c
24. c
25. b
26. b
27. a
28. b
29. a
30. c